The Way Home

Discovering The Path To Your Truth, Nature, and Inner Treasures

by

Vlada Zapesotsky, MA, PAT

ISBN-13: 978-1986792851
ISBN-10: 1986792854
CreateSpace Independent Publishing Platform Sunnyvale, CA

This book is dedicated to my beloved

parents, who created

the best home possible for me.

Contents

Preface

Before you begin this book, I would like to share with you what it means to me and the story behind its creation.

First, this book is my confession—in the sense that I have never been so sincere at any point in my life about my inner truth. Perhaps, I have never been able to be so, as I can today.

Second, this book is a dream come true. Not that I dreamt of writing a book my whole life, no. Simply, in the beginning of my journey, writing seemed nearly impossible and unattainable. This process required of me a great deal of faith in myself, in what I do, in my dream. Even though I had considered myself to have this faith, throughout the process of writing I discovered just how much I needed, and how strong my faith needed to be to make my dream come true. And, yes, I found that faith within me. Therefore, to me this book is a dream that came true thanks to the great faith.

Finally, this book is a vision in the sense that I had envisioned it as if I had already known it. I felt as though it all had been already written somewhere within, and I only needed to tune in, to "download" it exactly as it was meant to be. Nothing in this book is calculated or rationally planned. Of course, I had to structure and organize the written material so that it would not be a chaotic flow. At the same time, it was extremely important for me to preserve the book's natural, free, and clear energy without relying on external standards and norms—only using the vision that would appear inside me and conveying it without spoiling or falsifying it.

I can say that this book is written for everyone, but this is not the whole truth. I wrote this book for myself because the entire process of writing and the product was my journey toward myself, which, thanks to this book, became truly understood, clear, and accessible to me. Of course, I did not answer all my questions, nor did I uncover all the secrets. For this I give thanks, since the journey is only at its beginning and I have much more to discover.

This book has become my own personal bible, a compilation of my inner belief system, a map of what is truly important, precious, and true to me. This is a book to which I will return on many occasions to remind myself of what matters most and to fortify my faith in myself during moments of doubt. When I was writing, I, of course, thought of my children, of how I wish for them to have such a manual or guide—not to hear my advice or ideas, but for them to believe in their own Inner Home, in their truth, no matter how difficult such faith may be to find at times. Thinking of them, I kept writing even when my faith was under the siege of inner doubts, criticisms, and fears.

Yet, I believe that this book can be useful for others—precisely because I wrote it for myself. I am a human being who needs a feeling of Home; like most others. I am a person who needs not only a roof above her head, a warm bed, and food on the table, but also an Inner Home—the one that allows me to be myself, where I can live at peace with myself. It is important to note that nothing in this book is a general rule, law, or specific instruction—just as there is not a one-fits-all model of an Inner Home. The Inner Home is an individual, unique, and incomparable inner construction. Similarly, the paths described in this book are unique and true primarily for me. I can only hope that they will prove useful for someone else as well. I hope that this book brings inspiration and faith to everyone who reads it as it did to me in writing it, that its magical energy will help someone remember and feel anew the connection with his or her Inner Home. Most importantly, I hope that my inner choices will inspire some of you to start your own unique explorations, creations, and paths.

This book can be read in any order. None of the pieces of my journey have a chronological order—they simply happened to be told in sequence. You may begin anywhere you are led. But, most important, I ask you, my dear reader, that while reading this book, you listen to your inner voice and let it guide you through the chapters as if through a map, designing your own route and using this text to discover your true journey Home - to your True Self.

How could I leave this without acknowledgements? I have many to note, so, I will only mention the most significant. First, I thank my beloved husband, Arkady Zapesotsky, for his faith, for seeing the true me, for supporting me in all my endeavors, and continuing to do so unconditionally. I want to thank my wonderful children, Michael and Liel, who fill my life with incredible love and bring into it a true creativity. I thank my dad, who always insisted on truth and thus taught me to love the essence of being true, no matter how hard or painful it may be. And, of course, my mom for teaching me to dream and believe in wonders. I thank my sister, Valerie, who is the most genuine person I know. I also have a very large family that is dispersed throughout the world (Russia, Israel, the US, and other countries), whose support I feel every day, and to them I extend warm appreciation.

Along the way, several people in my life have become my true teachers: Svetlana Leontieva, David Bentovich, Kate Hudgins, and many more—to and for you, I give many thanks. When a book is 'thought, pictured, and spoken' in one language but needs to be written in another, it takes a very talented and sensitive translator to grasp its essential features. Therefore, my deepest appreciation goes to Galina Litvina, the translator of this book from Russian into English.

It also takes an exceptional editor to bring allow my vision to speak and yet bring it into clear language. In this I had Francesca Toscani, whose depth, experience, wisdom and spirituality created a wonderful and safe container for this book to grow and develop. Ronnie Gross is the creative artist who was able to take my verbal description of what I imagined and bring it to full color. I want to thank my friends— above all, my dearest and closest friend Anastasia Starikovsky, with whom I always feel at Home.

The list, of course, goes on. But honoring my promise to only speak of the most significant, I want to give the final thanks to my Inner Home, my soul, my inner world, and my personality who managed to express and convey all this in words.

Vlada Zapesotsky
Sunnyvale, CA
April 2018

Introduction

First, to explain and clarify the structure of this book, I draw you the map of the upcoming trip. This book is the internal story of a healing journey of self-discovery, the journey that brings the pieces of one's true nature together into a harmonious and genuine self. It starts with an imaginary story that activates your inner world and inspires before the journey. Then I introduce the guides and companions that will support you on the way, and to some helpful tools and resources that you can use and rely on throughout the journey. Along this way, you will hear my personal and professional sharing, see my discoveries, and visit my Inner Home. After that, you are ready to take action and explore different paths that can help you discover your own true way, pave the roads, and bring you home to your own True self. My hope is that at the end of this book, you will feel the desire and readiness for your own independent journey Home.

After the fairy tale story "The Way Home", I explain the meaning of "Inner Home" and "Soulful navigator" and how they work along the journey. In addition, I present three inner roles that are necessary companions and helpers on Your Way Home to your True Self.

The concept of the inner role comes from the psychotherapeutic method of psychodrama and represents certain inner expressions or parts of ourselves. Some common examples are: inner child, inner teacher, inner frightened little girl, inner wise man, inner controller, etc. We are full of these characters, colors, and expressions, and in psychodrama, there are many and various techniques that help us discover, recognize, and accept these roles, thus expanding our inner repertoire and acknowledging its complexity. In his "Role Theory", Jacob Moreno, author of psychodrama methodology, posited that when we allow ourselves to assume a certain role—or simply "try it on"—we awaken our imagination, character, and can even speak the text corresponding to that specific role. On numerous occasions, I was able to confirm the power of this theory in practice, when working with my clients and by participating myself in various psychodrama workshops.

The inner roles that I present in this book are the Prescriptive ones. This term was coined by psychologist and founder of the post-traumatic Therapeutic Spiral Model (TSM), Dr. Kate Hudgins. Prescriptive roles are clinically necessary and prescribed by the therapist to anyone working with a traumatic issue to help support them safely through the process. I, too, chose to prescribe and develop these inner companions, helpers, and guardians who can aid us in reaching our Inner Homes. Each of them has his or her own features, strengths, values, and purpose. Each is in the right place and knows what he or she is responsible for. Throughout the chapters, I share the messages of these characters so you can experience their presence and endow them with your unique traits, personalities, intonation. These inner characters live within each of us, and only you know how each should be speaking and presenting him or herself to help you personally.

So now that we have the map and the structure, let us begin with the story...

The Way Home

This story is dedicated to the child who lives inside each of us and waits for our grown-up self to help him/her to find the Way Home.

It is a mythical story about a boy. But it will not be about where and how he lived. Rather, it will be about what was going on inside him—his private, Inner Home. When the boy was just born, inside him was a vast open space, like the cosmos—infinite, undiscovered, mysterious, and magical. The boy's parents so wished to solve all the puzzles of that mysterious cosmic space, and they tried their best. But only the boy himself could make the true discoveries. Only he could reveal the laws of his universe, uncover its life, unearth hidden treasures, and find resources, strengths and inner powers. Only the boy himself could explore his inner universe and open it up to others. And, since this was such a huge task, he was given an entire life to do so. So, he began to live and every day brought him new discoveries. Each day he learned something new about himself and the world around him. Each day he acquired new feelings, thoughts, sensations, and experiences. New heroes were born.

At first, inside his universe appeared Mom; she was the center, she occupied the entire universe. She was the Creator of him and his world. The boy could not separate himself from Mom; all of his inner space was intertwined with her, and it was impossible to determine where he was, and where she was. So, he swirled in that space and was content and happy.

Soon, there appeared Dad and Grandma, and even a neighbor, who always waved at the boy and smiled—and from that smile something inside the boy awakened, something was unveiled to him. The boy knew that this something—if it had a taste, would be a little tingly and delicious. Then, one day when the boy was on the street, a vicious dog attacked him and a new room appeared inside his Home. And, although the dog was quickly calmed down, inside the boy an entire room of fear opened. Subsequently, there were many fears, and they constantly multiplied and mutated, and his Inner Home grew and became more complex.

But as his universe continued to grow, just as the boy was growing, other rooms opened up, too. Soon, imagination came to life inside the boy and he painted all his inner world in the different colors he was recognizing and beginning to love. He populated this universe, too, with new fairy-tale heroes, fantasies, and dreams. With every new day, the universe inside the boy spun faster, turning from one side to the other. Inside him, something was constantly going on, flourishing, fading, and awakening. And the boy followed all of this very closely—on the inside. He was very focused on that internal view; that is why on the outside it seemed that nothing was going on with the boy. He was still young and he simply did not know yet how to express everything that he saw on the inside—neither in clear thoughts, nor in words, nor in movements.

But only a few years later, the boy began to express his inner world, first slowly, then more and more. He shared his thoughts, openly showed his feelings, and played with his imagination. His inner space did not appear to grow outward because, since the very beginning, it was already infinite. The boy simply kept discovering inside himself new parts of that universe and now he learned to share them with those around him. Each time he felt something new, the boy tried to show his treasure to his loved ones and kept believing that they would understand and accept him as he thought he was. He did not know yet that when one shares something intimate, valuable, and very personal, not everyone around is just as attentive and careful or caring as oneself. Not everyone sees and hears things as one does himself. That is especially why he could not expect that those closest to him would begin to change. Soon they would begin to judge, belittle, criticize, and sometimes even frighten that beautiful being he had discovered inside himself and had shared so generously and openly. He did not know what was happening.

But still the boy kept listening to himself, kept trying to express himself to the people around him. Until one day a tornado swept right through him. We do not know for certain what caused that tornado, but it was clearly such a force that swept all aside on its way. And it burst into his beautiful, peaceful universe. That was the first time. Later in life, there would be a multitude of different storms—some greater, some smaller—and the boy would learn to deal with them, and even not to notice them. But that first tornado was completely unexpected to him, and thus ended up being the most destructive.

After that incident, the temperature inside the boy changed. From a humid, enveloping warmth it turned into a chilling and sleeping cold. Such cold that makes everything stiffen and want to stay still and not move. Better yet is to fall sleep under the mantle of such cold. And the boy did begin to fall asleep on the inside, as if his inner world had immersed itself in a foggy cloud; everything around him became blurry and lost all color. The boy's warm and loving heart became covered with an icy crust, and he was no longer hearing its tender and truthful voice, only a remote, muffled pounding. His beautiful, harmonious, and wise universe suddenly began to fall apart, and the tornado spun away all that the boy had discovered with such attention and love, sweeping away everything on its path.

Maybe that disaster was caused by the beautiful, clear light that radiated from the boy so openly and freely, illuminating everything around him. Maybe his light blinded something on the outside so strongly that it must cause either an earthquake, or a tsunami, or this tornado. It is not so important what caused that destructive force and why it struck the boy in particular, because our fairy-tale is about what happened not outside, but inside him.

When this terrible tornado struck, the boy was still little, but already very wise, and he realized that he needed to save himself and rescue at least what remained inside him. He knew he did not want to fall under the eternal sleep-spell. He understood that the only chance to survive was to run far away from those ruins, cracks, and the swirling chaos. So, the boy decided to escape from his inner universe to not see, hear, or know what was going on in it. He realized that the only way to survive outside was to forget about all that beautiful and harmonious universe that was his true, natural, and safe home. To forget about that tornado, the destruction, and the reasons for that destruction. It was only in this way could he endure the loss and continue to live and believe in any life. He even managed to convince his own mind of this, so that it would help him forget everything.

But still, he was a wise boy and before forgetting everything, he decided to hide away all of the surviving treasures, all of the undiscovered potential of his universe. He understood that these parts of him will know and remember the truth. That is why they needed to be stored someplace far away, beyond the line, beyond the boundary of his consciousness.

So, he sent all of the most precious and beautiful parts of his nature into the Neverland. He had heard of this Neverland and knew it to be the land of imagination, fantasy, and dreams. This is the beautiful land where the lost parts of him would be free and happy. They would be able to live there in any way they want, without rules, judgments, and reproaches. They will never grow up and will not meet a single adult, because they do not trust adults anymore. They will remain safe in Neverland—in his dreams and fantasies, and he will never bring them out again. His lost parts of childhood could only come Home again when it would be safe; only if at least one strong and wise adult would be present. This person would meet them with love, accept them the way they are, and give them a chance to grow and open freely and naturally. The boy was very clear about all this and he was satisfied.

Meanwhile, the boy himself would be able to visit them from time to time and each time that he would meet with them, it would be surreal, like in a dream—so he knew he could never believe exactly what they were saying about the outside world. But before the boy left his Inner Home to run as far away as he possibly could, he took one more look at the pieces left after the destruction. He now saw a lot of empty space that was formed after he hid away his remaining potential, and realized that, in order to continue living on the outside, he would have to fill that space with something. He decided that, most probably, he would fill this emptiness with something so foreign to him, from the world outside, something that would not remind him of his true nature, because remembering it was too painful.

Now was the time for the boy to take the last step to rescue himself and leave his true Home. But he did not know where to run, because he could not really escape from himself. So, he decided to run away into the outside world—where his sight, hearing, thoughts, and feelings would be directed outside, and not inside, like before. He no longer wished to see, hear, understand and feel his inner world. It was too painful and dangerous. He took a deep breath and leapt outside. Of course, from outside, no one noticed anything, and that was exactly what the boy was counting on. Once he was completely on the outside, he looked around and, to his surprise, saw so many interesting things that he did not notice before. He said to himself, "How much I was missing!?! Here is everything one could ever want. Ready. No need to discover anything. Just take it and use it."

To compare, the boy decided to look inside himself from the outside. But now it proved to be not such an easy task. And, now, he did not even like at all what he saw there. From where he was now, the boy could only see darkness inside himself. "You can't even see anything there," he said to himself, "An empty and useless space. I was busy with silly things, and what happened was my fault. Instead of soaring on the inside and just enjoying myself, I should have paid attention to what was happening on the outside. I should have felt that something was wrong and have stopped that tornado. I should have protected myself, but instead I marveled at that space that is really only a black hole!"

And that is how new creatures came to live inside the boy. And they were named shame, blame, and judgment. But, because they themselves were dark, he did not even know that they had entered...and he was already far from his Inner Home.

He was happy on the outside now, where everything seemed light and clear. Everything had its name and definition. It was possible to compare everything, to give an opinion on everything. It was possible to control everything. Not like on the inside. Now, everything back there seemed so mysterious, confusing, strange, even foreign.

One day, not too far into the future, the boy's heart was trying to tell him something from the inside, and, for a moment, it seemed to him that all this darkness was at once clear and familiar to him, like a native home. But right away he discarded this thought. It seemed scary to him, and he no longer wanted to be scared. Now he wanted to be sure of himself—stable, calm, and not asking unnecessary questions. He wanted to be an adult and know all about this world. So, that was the task he focused on.

The boy learned the ways of this outside world quickly. He began to listen closely to the adults (even when they thought that he was not) and he memorized things. Everything he heard around seemed important and correct to him. He was a very diligent student, and hence he took everything seriously, believed and repeated it. He wanted to learn all the laws of this world to finally feel safe, feel himself at home. But that feeling of Home, the feeling he had a faint memory of, was moving farther away from him with each day.

On those rare days when he let himself play with his imagination, with toys, or with friends, he felt as if he were transported into a wonderland where everything was easy and clear; it all made sense. He let himself remember, if only for a moment, that in that play land, he could be a wizard, a traveler, or even an evil dragon. He could go to battles, die and come to life again, fly and discover unknown countries. He could be whomever he wanted and not feel shame, not be punished, not be sentenced and convicted, because it was just a game. Though these experiences happened only rarely in his inner universe, he could feel the connection again to his True Self-Inner Home. As he got older, he went there rarely, and that world became dimmer. The boy returned again to his outside reality because it just was more difficult for him to play with his imagination. Soon, he completely forgot that it was possible at all.

But, in his outside world, the boy felt there might be something missing and tried his best to find that once so-familiar-to-him feeling of safety and, at the same time, freedom. He did not remember exactly from whence he knew it. "Maybe from childhood…", he thought. He would run to his parents, family, friends to find this safety and comfort, which calmed him for some time. But soon the boy would again begin to feel homeless and lonely. Unable to refuse, he tried everything that this world offered him. He was so afraid to miss something that would finally give him what he was looking for. So, there were moments when the boy felt tired and desperate. He felt as if he were running in circles and could not find the path that would finally take him Home, to that distant memory, to that feeling he had lost, which he began to call his True Self. So, in trying everything, the boy set for himself new goals, but when he reached them, he realized that he was mistaken again. He read books, listened to lectures by the wise people, searched for the answers everywhere around him. But somehow, he felt that he was not finding his real answer.

Only when the boy would close his eyes, after a minute of darkness, would he begin to see images, hear words, follow the story lines that intrigued him. And, this all seemed much more real than everything that surrounded him in his outside world. Sometimes he did not even want to open his eyes, so that the true life that was revealed from under the cover of the darkness would not end. And when the boy would open his eyes, he felt that he was still dreaming awake and it seemed as though no force in the world could lift the spell of this eternal sleep.

Time continued and things began to change slowly, almost imperceptibly, so that the boy could not even remember anymore at what moment he decided to look once again into that scary darkness inside. He only remembered that he felt an irresistible desire to learn the truth, no matter what it would cost him. He understood that he was ready for the truth now and he realized that such truth would not come from the outside. As soon as the boy accepted as a fact that his truth would not come from the outside, it was as if something inside him began to move. It stretched, yawned, and slowly opened its eyes—just as a baby wakes up after a sweet dream, satisfied and happy.

Gradually, the boy began to feel that inside him once again had awakened the senses of sight, hearing, smell, and touch. He suddenly felt that inside him there was real life, very true and deep, and that life was so much more important than everything that was going on around him. It was as if he remembered again his inner planet, his Home. He remembered that he had come into this world to explore and discover his universe, and that only he could do that. It was as if between him and his Inner Home an invisible thread stretched and pulled him back. All of this he remembered, of course, not in his mind, but in his heart and it was very difficult to describe those feelings in words.

Eventually, the boy clearly sensed that he needed to go. He felt that pull, that enormous longing for Home, and clearly understood that all that surrounded him at that moment was not home, but an illusion of one. And, he was not looking for illusions anymore because he was now ready for the truth. He did not quite understand where to go, or how he was going to get there. He knew he had to follow that thin invisible thread, seen only by his heart, until it would bring him to his true Home. He was impelled to go, believing that if he would just begin the journey, he would certainly arrive. The boy realized that it was very important to believe in the journey itself, in its meaning, and appreciate that he was finally going in the right direction. Then, everything that would happen on this journey would not be in vain.

This would be a long voyage towards the truth that was inside him. And he was lucky. Even in his outside life and with its experiences, he had gained all the necessary skills and qualities to withstand this journey. He was tough, patient, persistent, courageous, and hardworking. Having walked his short, but uneasy, path in life and having withstood it with dignity, he was ready for anything. He believed that after so much effort he deserved to reach the truth. He would not deviate from that path, whatever happened. Making the decision and assenting to the journey was exactly the moment his trek back to his True Self began. And, no matter how hard it was, the boy believed that he was finally on the right path.

While on the path, some changes started to take place that even surprised him a bit. He stopped comparing himself to the others, believing everything he was told, being afraid of his own darkness. The boy once again began to hear the voice of his heart. He perceived his own pulse, noticed his thoughts, listened to his body, recognized his feelings. The boy became more attentive towards his dreams, desires, and goals that were now leaping out of his heart. Inside him again was born curiosity, like in childhood, and he felt the importance of what was happening. He once again wanted to be an open and curious traveler who discovers inside himself new horizons and believes in them. That would mean that he believes in himself. And the more he believed in his journey, the more precisely his inner navigator worked (and what traveler does not need a navigator?). Located in the very center of the boy's soul, it was his special star; but, from such rare use, it had almost stopped sending signals.

Yet in that moment when the boy chose his path Home, toward himself, his navigator activated itself again and was guiding him more and more clearly. It showed the boy precisely where he needed to go, while selecting the safest, freest, and most natural path for him. This was so because a journey Home is always protected, cleared, and blessed—and the boy trusted this. At times, the boy wished to speed up his journey, go around an unnecessary traffic jam, or not stop one more time. But the navigator kept leading him down the exact way that was meant for the boy—the one that would bring him to his Home.

And then, one day the boy finally arrived, returning into his inner universe, into his world, his space, his freedom, his nature. The boy looked around and saw so much of the destruction, drought, hunger, and neglect. He did not recognize the beautiful universe that he had known from his childhood. But he saw it clearly now. Aside from the ruins and drought, there were piles of castoffs, randomly strewn about. The boy did not even imagine how many useless, unwanted items he had accumulated during his life, after he had left for the outside world. Now, he was seeing it with fresh eyes. There were mounds of ideas and laws unusable to the boy that he had acquired from the people around him; useless thoughts and beliefs that he had inherited from his family and the previous generations; unexpressed emotions and feelings that once were natural, but with time had become a stinking pile of waste that made the boy want to turn and run. Inside his once peaceful universe reigned violence. The inner universe was ruled by shame, blame and condemnation. It seemed that it had been impossible to stop those wars, destruction and disaster that happened with the storms that went through in his life. But he had been disconnected from his inner world so he really did not even notice. He remembered that there had been peace and happiness at this Home, his true self, which was now covered with this debris. The boy realized that it was not enough to connect to his inner world and recognize the traumas, but he must now discover the truth that lies underneath—the truth he hoped to find again. It seemed to the boy impossible to return the original, natural form of his universe or protect it from this endless oppression. He sat down on a rock and wept as he had never before, mourning everything he had lost in all those years—his separation from Home, loneliness, suffering, and the destruction that he had gone through. He wept over every piece of his inner world, every cell of it. He was feeling the unfairness of everything that had happened and realized that he could not turn back time. He was confused, dumbfounded, and lost. The boy no longer knew where to go and why.

And suddenly the boy saw that, from his tears the ground had become moist. From dry and crumbly, it became damp and strong. An instant later, a beautiful and rare flower grew in that spot. The boy knew this was a message. He smiled, rolled up his sleeves, and began to bring his planet back to its original form. He was no longer afraid of his tears because every tear generously watered the driest parts of his inner world, thus returning them to life. The boy used this magic, this return of life to give him faith, and he believed in his Inner Home as he did in childhood, with all his heart and soul. He knew that if he was loyal to his Home, if he did not abandon or betray it, peace and beauty would surely prevail. No longer did the boy want to run and hide. He was ready to descend into that seemingly impenetrable darkness. As a reward for his courage, his nature would bestow upon him light, of which there was always, albeit by a little bit, more than darkness.

While taking the steps on the path, the boy learned to no longer be afraid for himself. He knew that no matter what, here, inside, he could always feel safe. Here he had everything that he could ever need. He only needed time to open everything up again. And yet, the boy had managed to fall in love with that life outside, too. He wanted to use the entire experience that he had undergone on the outside, to bring it inside his Inner Home. And also, to express from the inside to the outside, everything that he wanted to since his childhood. The boy wanted these two worlds to meet. He wanted to retain all of those who were near and dear to his heart, whom he had met on his journey, and all those who had also come from the outside to form a part of his world.

A magical door—that is what the boy wanted to find that would open freely in both directions, through which he could walk calmly from his inner world to the outside and back. A door that would cover his inner world and protect it. A door that he could open to invite into his Inner Home those whom he trusted. The boy was sure of himself now and knew he would only open it to the right people, at the right place, and at the right time. He looked for such a door in many parts of his universe. One day it dawned on him that the door cannot be by itself; it cannot simply remain in the middle of his inner universe. Even though his inner world was unlimited, the door must still be a part of a larger structure, with walls and a doorway. The boy realized that no matter how beautiful and diverse was his universe, after all that he had been through he desperately needed a safe container with clear boundaries. This new container would now accommodate him entirely and would grow and expand together with him.

The boy also realized that even though his inner planet was the dearest place to him, he could not call it a safe and natural home yet. It was too vast and mysterious. He had been away from it for too many years. He had been through much in his outside world, but much had taken place inside since he was just a child. The boy knew that for many years he had not watched himself on the inside—it had been too dangerous and painful. And now, having returned to such a place of observation, he wished to create for himself the exact conditions in which he could remain inside. He wished to organize his planet without running away out of fear and without falling asleep from the cold. So, the boy began to build inside his planet the home that he needed; the home of his dreams; the home that wasn't invisible to those who look with the eyes. He would make this a special Inner Home, one that would only be possible to see with the heart.

In all his life, the boy had seen many different homes, but he knew for sure that the one that was inside his inner universe and that was the very center of his being, would not be similar to any of them. It would be a unique structure, built from his personality with all its parts, colors, experiences, and boundaries; a home in which his soul would be able to grow safely, freely, and naturally, a home where his true self can live and grow. The boy knew that his inner universe would always protect it. He felt and saw from the inside that around his home there was an infinite, cosmic space, and hence he could expand it and increase it as much as he wanted. He knew the building would never have to stop and he was very excited.

The boy wanted to make sure that in his Inner Home there would be space for memories, feelings, and experiences of his life on the outside because he did not want to forget anything anymore. He loved and accepted his truth and his story the way they were. So, he decided to create rooms for the pieces whose return he awaited—each forgotten and abandoned part of himself would want to come back Home, where it would be welcomed and accepted the way it is. With great love and care the boy created the kids' rooms for the pieces he had lost as a child. He prepared in them everything that his child parts loved and cherished so much. And next to each of these rooms he put as a guard his strongest and also most attentive adult part. The boy found inside himself enough adult strengths that could take care of the little ones. He told each of his adult parts which child it was waiting for and taught it exactly how to take care of this child.

For the boy, it was important that his home was not only truthful, but also safe. He wanted it safe so that in it could coexist his calmest, happiest, and most peaceful parts along with the most frightened, hurt, and belligerent ones. In his home there had to be space for all of them. The boy wanted every part of himself, his old and new, to receive the space it needed in this happy and peaceful new home.

Yet, there were moments when the boy would get tired and lose faith that all this was possible. Then he would step into the outside world, watch the people and the events around him, and realize how much everyone needs to have such an Inner Home. A home where everyone can live, and not just survive. It was at those moments that the boy would believe that if he, himself, can build such a home, then everyone around him would believe it could be possible for them too. He believed that he was building his home not only for himself, but for all the people on this big planet. The boy felt it was his duty, his job, his meaning, and importance in this world. This work called upon him and lured him back inside to finish the construction, no matter what.

Each time upon his return, the boy found in him new strength. He felt that he was not alone, that behind him were his helpers, his followers, all the powers of his inner and outer universe. His predecessors and ancestors, everything live that exists in the world. And soon, he saw that they began to gradually come home—all of his surviving pieces. He hardly breathed as he watched them come. They were returning from Neverland, from his dreams and fantasies. He believed those beautiful, pure, and whole pieces were the treasures he had once buried, his untapped potential, his true meaning and importance in this world. Soon, the boy's home began to sparkle in many colors, becoming warm, cozy, and safe. To his surprise, there was enough space for all of the residents—and all were welcomed with love, attention, and tolerance. The boy had made sure that everything in the home was arranged so that each part would feel at ease and free and would continue to grow.

Slowly, surely, the boy continued to bring his inner universe back to its natural form. He cleared out the trash, took care of the abandoned parts of his world, rebuilt the destroyed and distressed spaces. In one way, he was very pleased that his planet was going through a global warming because he remembered very well how hard it was to live in freezing cold. But the boy was also sure that his planet would again return to its natural climate—it would be the necessary and perfect temperature for him to thrive.

The boy relied often on his soul navigator who helped him move safely around his planet, find lost lands, explore new ones, and orient himself in his inner space better each day. He was acquiring new parts that he had discovered and bringing them into his home to live peaceably with the others. And the more the boy felt at home with himself, the easier, freer, and more naturally he could communicate with the people around him. He no longer needed to close up and hide from people and situations, looking for safety, because he was protected by the boundaries of his Inner Home. He no longer wasted so much energy and strength to achieve external goals and communicate pointlessly because he knew that what he needed was already inside him. The boy was open to the outside world and, because he was sure of himself, he knew when to open the door of his Inner Home, and only to those whom he trusted. He realized that even the kindest and most loving people are not always able to treat his inner space with care and respect, simply because they have not discovered all the value and importance of their own Inner Homes. Hence, they could unknowingly litter, bring negativity, or even harm the boy's home. He, on the other hand, already knew the price of the hard work he had completed and the importance of preserving his Inner Home. That is why he watched very vigilantly to make sure that his planet remained free, while he no longer gave into any more negative influences.

When the boy was focused on the people around him, studying with sincere curiosity the inner planet of each, in his home remained his inner observer, or Housekeeper. This Housekeeper was responsible for a neutral observation, not judging or condemning what was going on around the boy, but watching and telling the boy about it. Because everything that was happening inside him was important, that neutral observation helped him maintain communication with his home, even when his eyes and ears were directed to the outside. The Housekeeper also was responsible for the cleanliness of the home, sweeping out with exceptional thoroughness, those old feelings of shame, blame and condemnation. These feelings accumulated especially often in the corners of the boy's Inner Home when he communicated with people. But the Housekeeper guided the boy how to detect those unnoticeable, but very heavy feelings, and free his inner space of them in a timely manner—sometimes even before they sneaked in.

The inner parents always remained in the boy's home and took care of his childhood pieces that demanded particular attention while the boy was communicating with other people. They calmed the crying, scared, and feeling-queasy-children living inside the boy, teaching him as well not to turn away, but rather to accept them as they were. The boy knew that as soon as all his childhood pieces received the care they needed, they would begin to grow into wonderful, attentive, strong, and wise adults. Those grown parts that had gone through the pain of suffering, and had received the needed attention and care, were true helpers, not only to the boy but also to those around him. They were eager to help wholeheartedly, with great compassion, empathy, and true emotional support. Some of them became healers and wizards and helped the boy in his determination to alleviate the pain of others in the world.

The boy felt that with every day he was becoming stronger, deeper, more versatile and stable, softer, more vulnerable, and warmer. He stopped judging and comparing his inner world to what was going on around him and in the world of each person he met. He realized that his own world was unique and special and it made no sense to compare it to other unique and special worlds. He was just happy to explore, get inspired, and return Home, to his True Self.

The boy was no longer in an external search; he had returned to his true home, his nature, his truth, his meaning, his inner universe. He just wanted to live, express his endless cosmic potential, and yet feel at ease. Now he was ready once again to let himself show all his spontaneity and creativity, and to live in the here and now. The boy no longer lived in his childhood home, in the past, getting nostalgic or fighting. He was not building himself a ghostly, imaginary home, while looking for it in the future. The boy lived every day, appreciating the present, creating his world freely, naturally, and truly. The boy was no longer afraid to live.

This is the end of the story that is the beginning of an actual life. A story that intertwines a fairy-tale and everyday happenings, dreams and reality, curiosity and wisdom, journeys and homecoming.

Prayer for the Journey

Life seems so short and fleeting when it passes me by, when I am out of focus, lost, and far from myself. Yet, each instant can be so meaningful, filled, and timeless when I truly live it with my soul, body, and mind, when—

I am truly present in my own life; my soul is alive, fluttering free within me; my mind is calm, clear, and cool; my heart is open, warm and courageous; my arms are open for an embrace and touch; my feet are firmly planted on the ground, with my roots running deep towards the center of the world; behind my back my imaginary wings are wide open, ready to take me anywhere and protecting me and my loved ones from bad weather and misfortune; my third eye is open, and through it flows the energy of the entire cosmos and our common subconscious; my inner universe lives in peace and develops in a free and natural way; within me exists a safe, free, and natural Home where I constantly grow, develop, and mature, and I choose to be Home and am able to focus on the journey.

It may seem an impossible task, but I know for certain that it is possible. It is merely a question of making a conscious choice in favor of my true journey and focusing on it, because everything that happens around me is merely a reflection of this journey. A reflection that I sometimes see through a distorted and foggy glass, while the actual journey takes place within, where the most important, pure, true, and real happens. I only need to allow myself to make a choice in favor of my true, not the distorted, life; of my true, not distorted, nature; of my true, not distorted reality; of my true, not distorted Home. It is then that my attention shifts its focus from outside to within, and I fully live my own life—through my Home, my family, my love, my truth, my happiness, my spirituality, my reciprocity, my purpose, my treasures and powers, my nature, my universe. Living my own life does not mean living it separately, but intimately with my true self.

All I need is to become a complete participant of this journey, to simply tell myself, "I have fought, suffered, played, wandered, and traveled enough. It is now time to go Home." All that happens around me is very interesting and fascinating. There are many people who inspire me and make me wish I were like them. There are many places that beckon with their mystery. There are many skills I would like to acquire. There are many spaces where I would love to live. But it is time for me to go Home—to *my* Home.

My Home calls me, longs for me, is empty without me. Someone there is waiting for me, missing me. Someone there loves me and knows me better than anyone else. There, I am in the right place. There, everything is true and natural to me. There, everything is mine and nothing weighs me down. There are no conditions or definitions. There, everything is simple and profound. There, everything is aligned and spontaneous. There, everything is clean, and I am not afraid of any disorder. There, everything is full of purpose and meaning. There, I am me, and not someone else. There, I am not alone; rather, I am whole with everything living that exists in our universe. There, I am responsible for everything, but at the same time I am not ashamed of anything and do not owe anything to anyone. There, I am the protagonist of my life, yet surrounded with help, care, protection, observation, and love. There, I am Home.

I do not need to know what this journey will be like, or what awaits me beyond the next turn. There is no sense in building theories and predictions about where I will arrive or how a particular part of my Inner Home will look; whether it will be easy or difficult for me to walk this journey, or even in which direction I should walk. I do not need to know any of that. I only need to make a choice—a true, conscious, mature choice—and thus connect to my personal soul navigator that will lead me Home.

It excites me to know that I can deeply feel and be completely present in every moment of this journey. I can be a pioneer in my own universe: a creator, an alchemist, a shaman, a healer, and a clairvoyant—even a divine being with a human experience. I finally can stop being a wanderer and a guest and turn into the rightful owner of my Inner

Home. A Home where lives my soul, my truth, my real, whole, natural and genuine self.

The Journey Begins:
My Personal Helpers along the Way

No matter what your destination is right now,
you are always on The Way Home.

Finding My Inner Housekeeper

Prior to beginning any journey, we need someone who will look over the map and the route that will progress. That is why an observer, who could see a more complete picture, is a necessary part of the preparation and eventual trip. Only he (I would call it "he", but it can be "she" too) can turn our voyage from a senseless wandering into a focused journey Home—a journey toward our truth and wholeness. While on the journey, with our limited vision, we do not to know what is awaiting beyond the turn since we only see that part of the way where we are now. Our neutral witness, our guide, would tell us what is going on and fortify our faith in the steps we take. And, while we wander and search for the path, it is also very important to know that someone is waiting for us at home; that someone takes care and protects it while we're gone. It is important that this someone should know the real and true us, and believe that, no matter what happens, we are resolute to come Home. Our witness, then, will watch over us wisely and calmly and illuminate our way, like a guiding star that is always present. Some people call such an observer God, Supreme Intelligence, Guardian, the Big Brother, inner voice, intuition. I call him simply my Inner Housekeeper—he who protects my genuine and pristine truth, neutrally keeps an eye on my inner space, and watches over my journey Home.

Throughout history, people have attributed to their 'overseer' qualities such as those of Savior, supreme judge, an arbiter of Fates, the Supreme Prosecutor in the universe. Perhaps, this is the reason it is difficult for many of us to hear and accept the inner voice of a neutral observer who does not judge us or make us feel guilty, but simply watches our journey, communicating observations. Even persons who are not religious per se, tend to listen more to their inner judges, prosecutors, and defenders than to their inner neutral observers, who do not express emotions or judgements but only the reality of the way it is. Afraid or hesitant of neutrality, we often mistake a neutral position for indifference and, conversely, we might consider those who scorn, critique, or sometimes humiliate us, as people who love us or are concerned for us. Thus, even in our inner universe, there is often no space left for a neutral observer. Perhaps, being so used to bombastic personalities, we do not want, nor can we hear, his calm and reasonable voice, telling us honestly what he sees of our inner universe. If we were able, we would find him pointing to the necessary resources and assistants who could care for our inner housekeeping and eventually bring peace to our inner world and clear the Way Home. For all of us who wish to achieve this calm and orderly inner universe then, we must believe our Housekeeper and allow him to do his job. We need to give him authority, our belief and attention. In this book, I am asking readers to reach for such a place of acceptance and trust, to allow this important internal role—the Inner Housekeeper the freedom to observe and monitor its realm, so that our true paths Home can emerge.

As an aid, I will tell you my story or journey to that inner neutral observer and Housekeeper. I grew up in a remote Siberian town, where around me no one ever talked about meditation, mindfulness, or even of any divinity. Like all children, I wondered about God but, in my mind, He was some remote judge or observer, who would scold me for doing something wrong or send some, unknown to me, terrible punishment. I never perceived God as a defender or concerned protector but, rather, as some force that always watched me and looked for what I did wrong. I was certain that "It" would definitely find something bad in me. Of course, as a child, I could not come to such conclusions on my own but, most probably, I reached them under the influence of those around me. No matter the source of these thoughts and perceptions, I did not attempt to get close to such an external observer and cold judge.

So, for a long time, both in childhood and at a more mature age, I yearned and looked for a neutral witness and observer of my development and growth. I tried to find it in my mother, but she had a different role to play. Therefore, I had to seek that observer, unconsciously at first and then consciously, inside myself. Yet, the voice and teachings of my mother remained with me and in some ways helped create a split in, what I call, my two minds or brains or even voices. I remember how, when I was a child, my mother used such words as "the voice of reason." She often told me, "Be reasonable;" "Listen to your mind;" "This is not reasonable." While these words might sound a bit harsh to a child, such a voice of reason became a friend and advisor to me. As I got older, I realized that the brain my mother helped develop might be called the 'thinking mind' or what Buddhists call the "monkey mind." This mind included my physical ability to solve problems giving orders to different parts of my body, storing memory— everything that we traditionally consider the brain's turf to be. Yet, in addition to problem-solving, I also enjoyed just pondering and I would follow the flow of my thoughts wherever they would take me. These thoughts would become a rhythm, a jingle, sometimes even a full musical composition. I thought about the people around me, the world, the events in my life, my desires and dreams. As I realized later, this was my Higher Consciousness or the Super-Conscious Mind. I remember myself enjoying this "thinking" process, without getting any logical explanations or answers, rather just listening to this wise, calm voice within me that simply knows. But soon enough, as I moved through middle school (a highly academic school), I began overthinking and my reasoning brain became so overloaded with information and endless thought processes that its activity completely pushed out my Higher Consciousness.

Here is an example: When I asked my brain for answers to profound questions, it would recite a list of my previous experiences (mostly failures or dangerous situations), warn me about danger, turn on fear and pressure, and lead me into enormous stress. My poor, overworked brain did not have any fresh information to give me, only the index of what had happened to me, what had been processed and stored on the shelf of the subconscious. Alas, my brain could not give me the experience of knowing, so my head started to ache and feel guilty. From all that tension, impotence, and the guilt about a job badly done, I began to have horrible headaches when I was about 10 years-old and eventually they grew into serious migraine episodes. Simultaneously, my brain was working very well when it came to memory, learning new information, or solving specific external problems. In other words, it was fully functioning when dealing with all practical and logical problems that had specific conditions and only one correct answer, but not questions or issues of an emotional or philosophical nature. And, since I was straining my brain more with questions for which it did not have answers, it was doing its overall job worse. However, along with all this confusion, there were moments when I felt that connection to my inner wise and calm voice again—this Higher Mind that carried within it the experience of generations. While it did not always have the single correct answer, its answer did give a very clear feeling of the appropriateness of what was going on and harmony within the spectrum of the world's knowledge—such knowledge that I was not supposed to have, yet did. I then felt a clear connection between both my minds or brains. Most importantly, I felt this connection to myself, my Truth, my Soul, to who I really am. Those were indeed such happy moments!

From a wise and reasonable little girl, I turned into a young adult who tried desperately to deal with that infinite flow of external information and to find in it some meaning. That voice inside me often did not coincide with the opinions of those around me, but even when I did not express it aloud, it still provided me with a very grounded sense of calmness and safety. I have come to realize that this voice is coming from my True Self, my Inner Home. It does not intervene but keeps an eye on a vast inner world and helps, by its presence, each part of the system to do its job. It is the source of the free-flow of knowledge that already exists, accumulated from the totality of human experience, that has been described over the centuries by philosophers and other deep thinkers. All the answers that I would probably need are there in an immense cosmic net, akin to what we know now as the Internet. For me, it is not an emotional voice but a reasonable voice that has a knowledge of the whole universe—and it was with me from the very beginning. Its calmness has always been there as a lynchpin, but its message had been pushed aside by the reasoning brain until I began my search for my Housekeeper, who is for me, the Inner Supreme Reason, my Inner God or

Higher Power, who is beyond all personal powers and abilities.

The key moment for me on that journey was meeting Dr. Kate Hudgins, a renowned therapist and researcher. In the model of her work on trauma, she presented me with the concept of an Observing Ego, a neutral, internal psychological part that is not emotionally enmeshed with what is happening in one's psyche. I suddenly saw ever so clearly, that I needed to recognize and even name this internal part of me that would just observe what is going on and honestly tell me about it. This part is not influenced by the emotions and does not have answers to questions I would ponder. It would not try to change what it sees, nor judge it. It would simply observe. Without it, nothing would make sense; without it, there is chaos and a universe in which life cannot exist—a real life, meaningful and valuable.

So, with Kate's help, I recognized and accepted my Inner Housekeeper because I highly treasure my Inner Home, its inhabitants, and all that is accumulated. I value my Inner Housekeeper, who watches over what goes on and guides me about when and how I can use the forces and resources of my brain, my reason, my soul, or my heart. I learned to trust and today, all of them are working together, keeping partnership and respect toward each other. And if they should get into a disagreement or a conflict, my Inner Housekeeper would let me know immediately. Today I feel comfort that my Inner Home is under a watchful eye, giving it meaning, value, and consciousness. I have learned that, before heading into a new journey of self-discovery, it is important to listen to the observation of my Inner Housekeeper and think through the path I am on.

My Inner Housekeeper tells me:

Even when you do not see, hear, or feel me, know that I am right here, right now, next to you. I watch over you and your journey, even when you think you are completely alone. I observe how you make your way through the external layers and the worlds inside, toward your Inner Home, to your true nature. I see how hard it is for you sometimes; how you lose faith and hope; how you get confused and forget where and why you are going. I also see your strength and determination; how with each new day you get up and continue your journey, believing that today it will get easier or better, and that you will finally get, even if by a little bit, closer to your own self. I believe in you and that is why I am patiently waiting for when you will find your way home.

From where I stand and with my clear eye as your Housekeeper, I can see that you have the gifts and strengths to be your own natural self. You have already used those strengths at different times to feel your true nature, which is free, real, open, and alive in the moment. I see that each time you are connected to these strengths and gifts you feel fulfilled and in touch with a potential that rises from you and links Earth and Heaven—your cosmic potential. From all that I see and have seen, your soul navigator is alive and you can depend on it to mark your route Home.

Connecting to My
Inner Heart Companion

In ancient Egypt, the heart was considered one the most important organs in the human body. The Egyptians were convinced that people think and feel with their heart. That is why, after someone's death, during the preparations for the burial, they discarded the brain since they thought that the deceased will not have any use for it in the next life. But they would always preserve the heart, believing that it contains everything one needed for the reincarnation.

I, too, believe that without a connection with our heart, no great journey--especially one toward our Inner Home, our nature and truth, toward ourselves— can take place. Therefore, I would like to introduce to you another companion who resides within us and is always ready to help. I call him my "Inner Heart Companion". The concept of such inner heart companion was inspired by an extremely powerful and effective psychodrama technique called the *double*. It is one of the key technical tools used in psychodrama; one I love dearly and use frequently in my work. Double, by definition, "is the name for the role of a person who plays the inner voice of the protagonist or the co-character." In some methodologies, the double is also called 'the alter ego'. The double's function is to help the protagonist express thoughts and feelings that often exist on a preconscious level. The person taking on the role of the double positions herself beside the character for whom s/he is doubling and speaks the words that the character might not feel free to say or needs help in expressing.

In my practice, I often explain to my clients how various techniques work, thereby preparing them for their personal, independent application. The technique of a double is rather complex, requiring the use of professional terminology and previous preparation. (By the way, separate courses and seminars for future psychodramatists are dedicated to this technique alone). To simplify the language of this psychological process, I decided to name this inner voice very simply—the voice of my heart. This expressive voice of heart can grow into an internal role, a live and fully-functioning component of our inner world. Every inner heart companion is as unique and personal as is the voice of heart in each of us.

Connecting with the voice of our heart, we obtain not only a guiding, compassionate companion who helps us feel present in the moment, but also a heartfelt friend who knows us from the inside, accepts us the way we are, and walks every step of the way with us—without abandoning us or turning away. Since I am a woman, I will address my Inner Heart Companion in a female form. The voice of my heart companion speaks in the first person because she expresses my inner monologue, my inner "I".

My Inner Heart Companion is not a copy or reflection of me; she is that deep, warm, strong, and brave voice of my heart. She is the pulse of my heart that sounds in me at this moment. She allows me to connect to my body, my feelings and true beliefs. This is the inner voice that comes from my inner source of love, acceptance, and compassion. She expresses my most sincere and profound feelings, not trying to change them, but simply voicing them. Her great power is the ability to hold all of me, even my imperfections, limitations, vulnerability and insecurity. This inner role helps to open my heart naturally and freely with the whole variety of my feelings. Thanks to her presence, I can express myself safely and naturally, no longer needing to hide my sincere feelings, lock down my heart, or freeze my sensitivity and sensuality.

Perhaps an example will help here:

While talking with a friend, my outer personality is engaged and on an even keel. But then my friend says something that feels like a criticism. I do not recognize it at first but my inner voice notices that my body has tensed and, inside I hear her saying in an injured voice, *"What you just said hurt me."* Having brought this to my conscious attention, I realize it is true and I now have the opportunity to address this with my friend and clear up any misperceptions or difficulties.

If I had not developed a good relationship with my inner heart voice, this slight would have gone unnoticed and perhaps developed into a much more intense interaction or resulted in me keeping my true feelings hidden. My Inner Heart Companion nudges me to honesty and truth in all its variations and gives me a chance to be present in every moment of my journey, in the here-and-now. By becoming one with my heart companion, I will never again be truly alone, and my journey Home will be filled with sincere feelings, unconditional love, and beautiful company.

My Inner Heart Companion speaks:

I hear how calmly and evenly my heart is beating right now. I feel that my body is relaxed and my thoughts are concentrated and focused. I feel my excitement and impatience in anticipation of the upcoming journey. I know that I am scared and, at times, doubts torment me. I also feel my confidence and faith in the path chosen. I decide to trust myself, my truth, my feelings, my sincerity, my inner voice. I feel my heart's warmth, courage, vulnerability, and love. I feel my heart's desires and trust its wisdom. It helps me be present in every moment. I want to hear my heart's voice and feel connected with her at every step of my journey.

Hiring My Inner Personal Assistant

I trust and know that we all come into this world filled with an unlimited potential of resources and strengths, both within our Inner Home and beyond its boundaries. By beginning to discover those resources at an early age, we face various reactions on the part of the adults. These attitudes towards us will either preserve and fortify those resources in us, turning them into treasures, or devalue and weaken them in our eyes. If the resources and strengths discovered in us are being recognized (by ourselves or a trusted adult) and continue to be a part of our life, we truly become filled with their power and support. They help us to overcome on our own different life situations, ask for the support we so need from those around us, or help other people. But if our strengths remain unnoticed, unrecognized to us or to those whose opinion we value, they automatically move into storage in our Inner Home.

So often I noticed how difficult life circumstances help many of us to see once again how strong we truly are and how many unused resources we carry inside us. However, as soon as we get back on our feet, it may seem to us again that we are weak and incapable because now we are not in crisis anymore and so all these discovered strengths are going back to be unseen and unnoticed. Yet, it would have been so much easier to help ourselves and others, or ask for the assistance from those around, if we opened the storage of our Inner Home more often and audited our strengths, resources, and assisting tools. So many times, we do not have enough time to stop and truly appreciate what we have gained. We grab them on the go and rush ahead, without looking back, just to knock on our neighbors' door and ask for something that we already have; something that lies hidden away, collecting dust in a far-away closet, without us knowing. Yet, those strengths reside within us, waiting for that moment of truth when we will pull them out of storage and begin to use them according to their intended purpose; when we finally will appreciate their value. Otherwise all our accumulated knowledge, strengths, uncovered resources will turn into trash, garbage, or unrealized potential. Only by recognizing and acknowledging our own resources will we be able to observe a given situation adequately and to apply our strengths as needed.

When I realized this scenario, I decided that another internal role is needed on The Way Home. I call this part my "Inner Personal Assistant". We always need support, every day, not just in the moment of crisis, but especially when we are full of ideas, will, and desire to move forward. So, in recognizing the need for such inner assistance, I "hired" him/her, clearly defining the functions and responsibilities based on the specific assistance I would need at any given moment.

At workshops, I often use the "job interview" format when we talk about uniting with this inner role, giving the person playing the role a chance to clearly and precisely define his responsibilities and goals, establish specific conditions, and negotiate. Only when one feels that he has established and voiced his true needs of the moment and conveyed the task to his Inner Personal Assistant, the meeting is considered to be concluded and the "agreement" signed.

My Inner Personal Assistant is responsible for several crucial processes. First, he (or she) focuses my attention on a very important question that I must ask before beginning to move or starting a new process: "What kind of help and support do I need for this part of my journey?" Answering this question, I can feel what exactly I need at this instant to come closer to my Inner Home and have an opportunity to express my true self naturally, freely, and safely. Additionally, my Inner Personal Assistant helps me realize and recognize the powers, strengths, and resources already accumulated inside me. These can be intrapersonal (intrapsychic) strengths, that is, those that I can feel within me. For example, my patience, trust, diligence, sincerity, intuition etc. These can also be interpersonal strengths, or those that I discover in other people and the ones that make me stronger. For instance, the integrity of my father, the power of my mother's love, the kindness of my grandma, the creativity of my children—all these give me strength. Finally, these can be transpersonal strengths—those that are bigger than me and that give me the necessary protection, help, and resources. For example, the wisdom of nature, the signs of destiny, the power of the Universe, etc. give me power and strength when I feel them. My Inner Personal Assistant helps me recognize these powers and resources, gives them names, and brings them into constant use. I imagine, too, that it is this inner part that helps me accomplish and realize all that I discover within myself, sharing it with the world around. My Inner Assistant allows me to move forward and grow, turning the accumulated resources within my Inner Home into concrete steps, goals, and results. It is as if he or she connects me with the surrounding world, from the inside out, thus helping me to express my truth and connect it to external objective reality.

My journey toward this meaningful and necessary inner role was not easy. Even since I was a little girl, I had learned to handle everything by myself—not because I felt enough strength in me to do it or because I felt myself very adult and independent; rather, it was because I believed that others expected it of me. That is, if I did not want to fall short of the expectations of the people whose opinion I valued, I had to handle everything myself. Then, I would get praise, and perhaps even respect and love, from them. It was as if handling things on my own was an unspoken rule of good manners. I chose not to ask for help, not question when something was unclear, not formulate what specifically I needed. It was hard for me to receive. Instead, I learned to feel myself as a separate being with my own issues and problems. I learned to hide my need for someone's help; feel alone in my misfortunes. With time, I had begun to feel that nobody would be able to help me in my tasks, even if they wanted to. At the same time, I did not truly recognize and acknowledge my own strengths and resources, and as a result, often felt as a victim of the circumstances.

For a time, I took on the role of a fragile and helpless victim who does not want to impose on anyone, but makes one want to protect her and give her a helping hand. Yet, very often my request for help did not reflect my need for it. That is, my own mechanism for determining when I truly needed help and when I could handle the situation on my own, was completely out of tune and inadequate. In moments when my inner resources fell short and I simply should have admitted that I needed help, I kept on carrying everything on my own shoulders and bent under this load. On the other hand, in the situations when I could easily handle myself well, I suddenly began to play overly-modest, complain, convince everyone of my helplessness, and accept help that often did more damage than good.

Only with time did I realize what kind of trap I was in. I simply could not determine which internal and external resources were at my disposal, when and how I could use them. Only in critical situations, some natural mechanism inside me would click, and each time I would be greatly surprised by my own endurance, strength, courage, and wit. So, one day I asked myself: "Do I really want to live my life like this?" "Do I really want to deal with occasional crises, drama, and troubles just so I can prove what I am capable of?" I realized how important it was for me to remember my own strengths and resources, because each day brings completely different confrontations, experiences, inner and external work. Moreover, I no longer wished to deal with all this by myself. I wanted to feel and clearly hear my internal helpers and, if necessary, to ask for help from the ones around me openly and freely.

So, I decided to populate my Inner Home with my internal helpers, having discovered and acknowledged their strengths and learned each of their names, so that I would know for certain when and whom I should call for help. However, it was not so easy to accomplish since they were hiding from me in the farthest and dustiest corners of my inner world and did not wish to show themselves. I realized that starting to see my inner strengths would be very difficult and I needed the help from those whom I trust and respect, who can see those strengths in me, and thus make them visible to me. It was important for me to look at least one such person in the eye and see in them a reflection of my own abilities and resources— to see that someone believed in me and my strengths, even when I did not.

So, I began to look around. I looked into the eyes of my husband, my children, my best friend, my colleague, my therapist. I called upon my imagination to envision my inner treasures, my irreplaceable inner strengths: And I found each one of them at the right moment. I discovered in myself wisdom, intuition, endurance, determination, light, truth, love, and courage. I met my inner mother, warrior, spiritual guide, healer, wizard, and many other parts of my personality. When the universe inside me once again was filled with strength, energy, resources, and mutual help, I was able to see how much support there is around me as well. I came to value anew the strengths of nature; I sensed protection of energy; I felt support from generations long gone. Around me, I saw people who wanted to help me not because I could not handle things on my own, but because they were simply happy to help me. I finally realized how many people I could help.

Even today, there are moments when I forget my inner and external resources and strengths and continue to feel myself alone against the entire world. I still sometimes drive a situation to an extreme, only to have my inner resources jump out and manifest themselves. Those moments are when the support of my Inner Personal Assistant is absolutely necessary. With his assistance and recognition of my inner strengths, I feel this big and strong world inside me and a connection to this big and strong world around me. My Inner Personal Assistant reminds me to take the inventory of my Inner Home more frequently, to discover newly acquired knowledge, experiences, strengths, and resources.

When I recognize that specific conditions and rules may change and be renegotiated, then the relationship with my Inner Personal Assistant grows and deepens every day. Most importantly, at any moment, I know where I should go to ask for help and support. I can recognize people around me who are willing to provide true and sincere assistance and support and I can feel my own abilities, strengths, powers, and resources. Today, I am able to rely on myself, openly accept support, and, therefore, help others.

A message from my Inner Personal Assistant:

First, I want to remind you that you have been through a lot in life. You have endured many complicated and difficult situations, yet you made it through. You are here now because of all that is inside you, and thanks to everything that is around you. You are ready to keep walking and continue on your path.

I am here to tell you about your powers, abilities, resources, life experience—all that you have accumulated within your Inner Home over the years and brought with you into this world. I am ready to support you in any of your endeavors or ideas. I am here to provide the help necessary because I believe in you, in your dreams, goals, and actions. I can help you build your circle of strengths, where you will be able to grow, develop, and express yourself naturally, freely, and safely. I can also help you see the circle of safety that exists around you—those people whom you can ask for sincere help and support. I am here, inside you. I am always with you!

Activating My Inner Soul GPS

I have always felt that inside me there is a wise and amazingly precise mechanism that helps me to be at the right place at the right time and never to lose my path. As soon as I took a wrong turn or remained somewhere for more time than I should have, I immediately, and almost physically, would feel something push me ahead, as if to remind me that I had gotten lost or distracted. It is as if inside me there is an unknown, but true route that suits me personally—my true path. This path is most natural, free, and safe for me. It is natural because it is as genuine to me as nature itself; it is free because it is always open and only I move down this path; and it is safe because, while I walk down this path, I feel that I am in my rightful place, following it toward my Home, toward myself.

It does not mean that this journey is easy, comfortable, or simple. It may be full of adventures, struggles, hard work, and patience, but as I go down my path, I know that I am moving in the right direction. I feel that my movement is in sync with the invisible inner mechanism-navigator-compass that comes from my very soul. My movement coincides with my built-in inner route, and I feel peace in my soul, incredible happiness, meaningfulness, and faith in my path.

I am not alone in this, but sincerely believe that such an inner navigator is in each of us since the moment of conception and the first days of our lives. Each of us is capable of perceiving this inner direction that is especially clearly felt in our childhood, when sensitivity and openness of the soul allow us to accept the signals of this navigator, without doubting or disputing them. Throughout life, we become distracted by the external noises, or by those that intrude and gradually turn into our inner noise screen. Eventually, hearing the signals of our inner navigator becomes more difficult, yet this mechanism does not get weaker and does not lose its functionality and precision. Nor does it lose its relevance and truthfulness. All that is required of us is to simply believe in it again, turn up the volume of our inner voice that, with instant precision, can determine whether we are walking away from our true path. It is the very voice that, when we hear it, we may feel angry, betrayed, or lost, because we then realize that we had taken a wrong turn, we had lost our path, we had betrayed ourselves. It is also the voice that brings peace and clarity, because it is always truthful and accurate. It brings us back on the right path.

So, when this inner voice grows within me, breaking through all the noisy static and obstacles accumulated over the years, and I again allow myself to hear it, my inner soul navigator reactivates with a whole new strength and begins to direct me toward my truth, my Inner Home. I do not need to know where exactly I am going, what waits for me at the turn, and what my journey will be like. I can only sense that I am following my path and that it will invariably take me to my Home, to my true self.

The inner voice coming from my Inner Navigator speaks:

When you go down the path toward your Home, your journey will be happy, meaningful, and blessed by all the forces of the Universe. If you set your Inner Home as the main and final point of your journey, it will not matter in the least how many stops you make on the way or how many extra turns you take, or how much traffic, accidents, or tribulations you face. You will find your Way Home and get there.

This route is built into you, and your destination is known from the start. You do not need to put an effort into following this route, focus on it, or think about each step you take. You only need to allow your inner mechanism to guide you, responding to its inner signals and trusting its correctness and precision. All that is required of you is to restart your inner program, make a conscious choice in favor of your Home, and repeat this choice every day, every minute—for as long as it will take to make it a true-life practice.

Then, you will be able to continue down this path, with calm and peace in your soul, happiness in your heart, clarity in your mind, and strength in your body. You will know that your inner soul navigator is taking you where you need to go and believe that your inner compass will invariably take you Home- to your True self.

The Journey's First Task: Building My Own Foundation

No matter what your destination is right now,
you are always on The Way Home.

On the Way to My Natural
and
True Foundation

Picture the following—you are building a house. Of course, you start with the foundation. You need wood, stone, and many other things. You have none of them, simply because you are barely starting your journey as a builder. So, you are willing to accept almost anything someone gives you. And all the people in your family give you all that they can share. Their intentions are sincere, and they are trying their best to help you. And so, they bring everything they have, dumping it into a single pile, without looking at whether you need it—but, again, all this comes from their hearts.

You work your way through the pile and find that there are nice and sturdy timber pieces that you can use to build. Then there are completely rotten, destroyed, weak pieces of wood with which you absolutely cannot build anything. Others may be perfectly good pieces, but they do not fit your construction in any way—maybe they would be great for a different house, but for yours they are just a disaster. And so, you start suspecting that maybe you do not need everything from this pile, but you do not have any other materials within arm's reach, and you do not know when you will get your own. On top of that, you feel somewhat awkward—your loved ones are bringing all this to you with good intentions, they are giving you the last of what they have. You do not want to offend anyone; you want to believe that the family knows best what to bring. If you do not believe your own family, whom do you believe? Besides, you so want to finish building the house as soon as possible, see it complete, move into it, be big and independent in your own home, that you close your eyes and ears at all these visible and invisible dangers and resolutely keep on building. Building and believing that everything will work out for you. And this faith helps (the faith always helps) especially in such difficult an endeavor as building a house.

However, even as you are building, the house begins slowly to sink, and in some places even fall in. But you keep on anyway. Floor after floor, room after room. And everyone around you pushes you onward, especially the family, "Come on, so much effort has already been put into this!" Everyone is anxious to see the result of all this effort. But of course, it is you who rushes you more than anyone else. Because you are in an unforgiving debt with your family; you built your house with their treasures. So, the only way to pay them back is to build an impressive, large house, one that will not leave you embarrassed. What is inside is not so important; the main thing is to make the outside look decent. Or, at least, no worse than the any others. Meanwhile, this house becomes more cumbersome and there are fewer chances that it will not come crumbling down. But, as you work, you try not to notice; you believe that if you paint a little here, file a bit there, fix here and there, then the house will survive, and you can finally even live in it.

But deep inside, you do notice and you are in a quandary as to how to address its problems. It is not that you are stupid or lazy, but for a good job and a house that you can eventually live in, it turns out that you need to start again from scratch. You must take the whole house apart brick by brick and replace the rotten wood foundation with new, strong timber, suitable for your needs. You ask yourself, "Were all these efforts in vain? Can it be that after so many years I have to start from scratch?" On top of that, you look at the others and say to yourself, "Theirs are already standing. No one knows how they built it, but it is standing. Maybe mine will withstand, too." You want to believe this, fantasize, idealize. And you really do not want to admit the truth because it seems wasteful to destroy what has already been constructed in order to get what you need. Even though only facing this truth can help you fortify your house and build it on its own natural and true foundation that is suitable for you and the way you live.

So, the questions you face are: How you can reinforce or replace the foundation without destroying the whole building? How can you sort out the materials that do not work for you without insulting the intentions of your loved ones? How can you allow yourself to build your own Inner Home while remaining within the family?

Bringing this metaphor into life, I believe that many go through such restructuring in their adolescence, when they have enough courage and desperation to take on the status quo. Many teenagers throw in their parents' faces all that was forced onto them or given to them without their consent. However, not everything at this age is perceived adequately and truthfully. And some realize that it is possible to review and revise one's Inner Home while not losing the loved ones, but rather distancing from them for a while.

Unfortunately—or fortunately—I did not go through this stage in my adolescence. The reality that surrounded me was too wobbly for me to construct my Inner Home on top of that. I just needed a sanctuary, a support, and I sincerely wanted to believe that inside of my childhood home, my inner self was safe. Only later did I realize that my first home reflected barely a part of me, of my truth. The vast part of my personality could not appear on top of the foundation on which the home of my childhood was built. But in my teen years I was too busy for a restructuring. It only began when I got married, very young at 20, and received a safe space for my own restructuring and transformation. Between my husband and me a true, strong feeling arose that continues to grow even today. The desire to get married seemed very natural to both of us. Yet, I think that some part of that decision on my part was linked to the irresistible desire to finally build my own home, have my own family. A home that would stand on my base, my values; built with my own efforts, and in which I would be able to finally be myself, decide, choose, express my opinion openly, without fearing the consequences. And most importantly, I would be able to feel that this is my home, truly mine, and in it there is a place for my own, unique construction and design.

When I finally got this very own space, I automatically began to reconstruct in it everything that I often saw in my childhood home. And some processes I even began to build to be completely opposite, assuring myself that by creating them opposite to what was customary in my parents' house, I am finally doing it my way. But none of that was completely true for me. Also, my new independent home and my own family did not make me free and truer to myself. Inside, I kept living in my parents' house, argued with them or, on the contrary, longed for their attention. I still lived through the relationships in my first family, its interests, its problems, its contradictions. In other words, I was neither building my own home and having my own family, nor was I still close and reconcilable with my first family and childhood home.

Much time had passed, during which many unnecessary thoughts, ideas, rules, beliefs, suppressed emotions and feelings came out of me, before I finally began to feel and realize what it was I really wanted—

what kind of home I myself wanted to build, what kind of family I would have. And it had nothing to do with my family being better, more correct and harmonious than the one in which I grew up. It was that now I could finally allow myself to build my own relationships, rules and processes, my true reality. I was able to create my own little world where I would truly feel at home—in a house where I myself want to grow and develop.

Only when I was able to create honest and safe conditions for my personality, could I express myself naturally and openly as a mother and a wife. By allowing myself to create a family that was truly mine, I was able to accept and understand the rules and processes of my parents' family and became more natural and free in the roles of a daughter, a sister, and a granddaughter. I no longer needed to run away from my first family, argue with them, or play only by their rules. I was able to become close to my parents, without idealizing them as I did in my childhood, but accepting them the way they are; to perceive clearly how we and our opinions were different. I then sensed an enormous and sincere gratitude for what we agreed on as a family.

The process of my inner restructuring is still going on—a process that cannot be done in a rush, on the fly. I do not want to simply deconstruct my entire building, returning to parents all that they had given me with so much love. I just want to be true to myself and to the family that I am building today. I want to hear my truth, while maintaining a connection with all that I inherited from the previous generations. I carefully treat anything that needs a restructuring or even a transformation so it can still become my resource and my strength, if only I can correctly recognize this precious material and make it useful for my home. I do this not because I feel awkward returning it, but because I really do recognize its value and uniqueness.

During this honest restructuring, I did not lose my family; rather, I said 'goodbye' to the idealized family from my childhood. And, subsequently, I gained two real and very special—I would even say, unique—families. One is that of my parents, and the other is my own. Now, I not only know, but feel, all that happens within my family is my responsibility, not my parents' or someone else's. And since my Inner Home has become true, I can allow myself to be alive and spontaneous in my physical home and my family. I no longer need to hammer in the big nails of the foundations and rules in order to fortify my family home. I simply protect its borders. I allow myself to develop, constantly extending the boundaries of my Inner Home, together with my family. I can calmly and gratefully accept what my parents and other members of my family want to bring to me with so much love, because I am no longer afraid that my own construction will come undone. Today my home, inner and outer, stands on a foundation of truth, and hence is strong and stable. Most importantly, I now know for sure how essential it is to have an opportunity to build your own true home inside the family. Because of this hard-earned knowledge, in my today's family, each person has a right to his or her own true construction—one that would allow him or her to feel truly at home inside our larger family home.

This message from my Inner Housekeeper helps me keep a true perspective:

Your today's family is the safest space for expressing your spontaneity, your individuality, your nature, both spiritual and human. You have walked a long and challenging way in order to allow yourself to be truly natural within your family, with your human limitations, unique abilities, strengths, and weaknesses. This journey of recovering your feeling of Home was possible only after you had taken apart your inner construction and gotten down to the foundation built by the family in which you grew up. Only then were you able to fortify your inner foundation with materials that are true and natural to you— what makes sense and has value to you. Only then had the foundation of your family become safe for you, because it was chosen and understood by you. Your family room began to be filled with incredibly bright colors, unique aromas, and a special home-like atmosphere. That family room in your Inner Home was no longer just a function or space that had to be planned, ordered, and filled. That room has become the most natural place for your growth, self-exploring, consolation, calmness, creation, and love in its greatest and most beautiful form. This is the room where everything connects for you—the heaven and the earth, the spiritual and the human. This is the center of your inner universe and your Inner Home.

On the Way to Freeing Myself from the Inner Cage of Illusions

Inside each of us there is a room where we keep and, sometimes even treasure, our illusions and disappointments about the home in which we grew up and the people who were around us then. We tend to either praise, please, idealize, and worship those people, or to deny, criticize, and reject them. It takes much courage and faith to agree to release ourselves from this room and allow us to see our own parents in their true light. This means to accept them exactly the way they are, without judging or living in a false feeling of connection and intimacy. Their role in our story is so great that in our lives we may be caught between two choices—to glorify or condemn them—because we feel that it is they who are responsible for our first universe, hence for who we truly are. They are our creators and first observers, and the very essence of our existence depends on how we perceive and interact with them.

But we often forget that there are more pieces to our story, that our first home was actually inside our mother's womb, and we can only imagine where our souls had been before that. Regardless of which home we find ourselves in upon our birth, our first memory and knowledge about who we truly are was created by our life inside our mother's womb. Even when the pregnancy was not safe enough or the mother did not take care of herself, we still had moments of feeling this safe and natural container where we could simply be who we were in that moment and grow at our own pace. As adults, we are so used to, and even trained for, suffering that it is not easy for us to accept the fact that, as an early human being, we were free, natural, and safe. Each of us is the highest form of creation and nature, which does not depend on us doing or creating something, but rather living freely and naturally, contained and expressive.

It might be somewhat disconcerting to accept this idea. When it first appeared to me, I was upset because I realized the difficulty not only in understanding this concept, but truly to feel it and even be it again. I had to admit to myself just how much my inner space had shrunk and decreased throughout my life and how far away I had gone from myself, from my essence, and from my pristine nature. I slowly allowed myself to acknowledge that I already had my first physical home and it was the womb. Therefore, even today, my body has these moments of memory, being natural and contained, because it is not about the mother/my mom and the way she accepted me; it is all about my truth and a feeling of a true Inner Home.

So, as I let myself remember this feeling of Home, I realized that I felt safe because I was surrounded by the womb, a unique, protective space, and I was strongly connected by the umbilical cord that was giving me life without demanding anything in return. The more I grew, the bigger the space around me was becoming. Nobody from the outside world interfered with my inner space. It was a home where it was safe to grow and be in my natural state, be my true self. And even if someone on the outside was trying to evaluate me (exams, doctors), it did not influence my form or perception in any way. I kept living and growing full force, independently of who thought what about me. I was at the center of the world, connected and present, and that world around me was my home. I believe it is the longing for that home where I could grow and be my true self that kept me restless in my later search in life. Yet, because I am a true believer, I kept believing that I can feel Home again and recreate this natural, contained, free and creative environment for my adult and mature self.

However, for an extended period of my life, I was living in an inner small room that developed from all the illusions and disappointments. I believed it my home, complaining of its inconvenience, injustice and tightness. My journey of releasing myself from this inner cage and consciously choosing the way toward my true Home, began when I decided to be brave enough to hear the whole story of my inner being, from the very start. This story was not always pleasant, sometimes it was dark, scary and painful, yet every piece of this picture was a true treasure for me, because with every step, I felt more real, alive and present. In this chapter, I share with you some of these pieces, that were very important for me and my eventual release and growth.

I was lucky to be born into a family, where I was expected and loved. My parents worked hard to build a wonderful home for me, and I am grateful that I was born and grew up with them. Yet, my childhood home could not substitute for me that natural, free and safe space that I remembered with my senses and that called to me so much. It seems that at different moments I knew that my true home was now inside me, and I remember myself hiding there my truth—my true feelings, thoughts, dreams, desires and discoveries. So, the reality that I knew was that I had wonderful parents who did the best they could to take good care of me. The truth that I did not want to see, and it took me a long time to discover, is that, in my childhood home, I did not always feel safe to be my true self, to share my truth, to express myself freely and naturally, and to grow up in my own pace and rhythm.

As I grew and matured, I adjusted to the home of my childhood and eventually I reduced my inner world to the size that was acceptable to those around me. In other words, my growth was on the outside and physical; on the inside I moved from an unrestricted, free and natural universe into a small room-cage, where I felt myself comfortable enough, or not worse than the other children around me—and maybe even better. Yet, beyond the limits of that room there was a magical world of fantasies, dreams, and freedom. A big beautiful world. Back then I did not know yet that this world was also inside me—that I would just need to open the door of the cage, step outside, and I would be there. But that step, that one simple step, requires a lot of courage and I would need a lot of strength, time, and faith to make that step.

During my childhood and adolescence, I was merely looking at that world through a small window, and sometimes I could even open it and breathe in the air of freedom and love—so fulfilling and unconditional. But many times, some adult would close it right away, telling me that there was a draft and I could get sick, fall, or even fly away in an unknown direction, propelled by this wind. It was scary to hear that. And soon I learned myself to close that only window very tight, observing all the safety measures, so to speak, which brought even more approval from the adults. What a responsible and independent girl, and I lived in an Illusion of safety, comfort, tranquility, acceptance, home.

Interestingly, everyone around me was telling me that this tight cell was the real world, and that what I had seen through the little window were nothing more than fantasies and dreams that had no place in the real world. Yet, much of what was going on in that room was an artificially-created, well-rehearsed play, but away from that room, in my free and natural inner space, there was truth and treasures—my real nature, desires, dreams, talents, and resources. So, I buried my most precious treasures very deeply hoping that no one would find them, take them away, or take possession of them. Some of them I had buried so well that I, myself, forgot where they were, and some I had forgotten completely. This was how my memory and my subconscious were helping me deal with my inner prison—they were telling me, "You are not missing much. Beyond the limits of your little, cozy, room-cage lies the unknown, but inside it is comfortable and, what is more important, familiar."

Of course, it is possible to break any system by force. It is possible to push very hard from the inside and then, at some point, the door will open under the pressure. It is also possible that circumstances and people could pressure our cage and we would jump outside just to survive, forgetting about fear, injuries, and the unknown. Many people say that this self pressure is a show of force and that we are brave in facing a challenge, a barrier that needs to be overcome. But for me, the true challenge and courage is when I stand at the door and, with all my strength, try to open it *and* it does not give. Yet, I stand there still, believing that I will find a way to open it, without pressing or forcing myself. I wait, gather my strength, and open the door exactly when I am truly ready to do it, choosing to be kind and gentle with myself. So, for me, waiting and believing are the true challenges. And while I waited patiently, I could study this space, discover where the light is and illuminate my little room so that its light began to spill beyond its boundaries and clarify other spaces next to it—those which were still not accessible to me. They were no longer dark, but now clarified, and I could walk into them with excitement, without fear. Step by step.

For a very long time I studied that free natural inner space, that was beyond the wall, in my imagination. I imagined many things about myself, staying in touch with my true Home. Fantasies and imagination are with us and our way of connecting to this inner space from childhood. I also fantasized of seeing in my parents the people who would help me recreate my true Home (the one where I would be just as free and protected as in my mother's womb). But they were wonderful people who, to the best of their abilities, were creating the home that seemed right— to them. A lot of time passed before I realized that, after I was born, I would become the only one who could help me return to my true Inner Home, to my truth. My parents could only bring me closer or farther on this journey, but they could not, in any way, walk this path for me. I accepted that it is not their fault or an unfair turn of events. This is the Way. The way it is supposed to be. That only I can start on a journey to becoming myself, to come back to my True self.

When I became a therapist and began working with families, I realized that another complication arises because many parents themselves have also gotten lost on the way to their Inner Homes. They may believe that their role in their children's lives is so great that this weight of responsibility crushes them. It does not let them breathe freely in a role of a parent. Some may actively begin to educate their children; some, conversely, may run away from parental responsibility. Some try to control; others leave things to chance. How sad that many do not realize that, in truth, parents are their children's conductors to and through this world. Their job is to give the opportunity to remember that first feeling of the Inner Home—that safe space where children can be natural, free, and accepted.

So, yes, we have this internal space where we can grow and develop at our own pace and rhythm, without adjusting to anyone, but trusting our own nature. As parents we do not create such space, but rather let us not forget that feeling, not squash it, and then, with time, we can express it and share it with the outside world. The parent role is a very important role that brings much responsibility, but it is a role of an observer and a conductor—not of a warden, a mentor, a protector, or even a creator. Only when I was able to see my parents' role in my own story as conductors and observers—fulfilling this role of theirs for better or worse, and bringing me closer to or farther from my Inner Home—could I finally step out of that space of illusions and disappointments and continue my own journey toward my Inner Home. This is the Home that no one can give or take away, because it is inside, always there. In it, there are many parts, colors, and tones, some of which have already manifested, while others are still idling. But most importantly, my Home keeps a memory, the very first memory of myself. It remembers how I was intended by nature; it remembers that my soul, compared to my tiny body, was immense. My first home in my mother's womb was filled with those memories and the truth about myself has stayed within me forever. I just needed *not* to resist the force that wanted to pull me Home, back to myself and the world inside. It was then that I could keep growing to develop my nature spontaneously, in the here-and-now, freely and safely, while expanding the space around me. It was then that I was able to break from the confining cage.

A message from my Inner Housekeeper stays with me and gives me confidence:

I see that when you follow the light, you always know where to go. You know what to do. Quietly and safely, you listen to your heart. It is necessary to begin the journey in an illuminated space, where the light is shining bright. This is not a one-day process, nor is it a trick. It is a life executing the art of small steps, each to be taken in the here-and-now, gradually proceeding toward Home, toward your True Self and away from illusions that encage you.

Slowly you approach the door and gently you open it, coming into your own light. Nothing brusque here; nothing forced. Gradually and lightly you substitute your illusory inventions with your true, real Home, where you can be natural, free and safe. You exhale and live.

On the Way to the Bigger Me

During my childhood and adolescence, I have had this feeling that there is a lot of me. Even too much of me. More than someone can handle. The hardest part is that this sense comes with a shame and blame self-talk—all my fault because I gave freedom to my feelings; that I was not modest and reserved enough, attentive to the feelings of others. I was greedy and took too much space and did not leave any for the others. I am guilty of having expressed myself completely, with all my temperament, emotions, and energy. I am guilty of inconveniencing someone. It is my fault that I was disrespectful to the person next to me who does not want or cannot handle all of me, etc.

Yet, deep inside I also had this vague feeling that I am not doing anything wrong. I am not trying to strain someone purposefully or to get into his or her private space. I am not trying to hang myself with all my inner weight onto that person. I am just trying to be natural, to be myself, to be as big as I can be. Now I understand how expansive and true this feeling was. But back then, I needed to survive in a society with its norms and laws. I needed to fit into an appropriate social picture that has one-size only. I learned that if I can squeeze myself like a spring, presenting myself in the format and size that are pleasing to the other people, then I am a successful, socially-active person, accepted by my family and friends. It would seem as if everything would be great.

But no, sometimes this does not work, because the spring inside cannot be constantly squeezed and in the most inconvenient moment it will release. Everything that had been accumulating inside now springs onto the outside: grudge, humiliation, endless effort to control one's self—or, from another perspective, manipulation of one's self; the feeling of injustice, betrayal and abuse of one's nature. All these feelings are true because that is what really happened inside of me.

One of my blessings is that I was always willing to talk to myself, to find a way to understand myself better, even in the hard times, so I looked for people, books and other sources that could support me in this honest self-talk. Sharing this feeling of being "too much" with people around me, I found out that many different people have felt this. I realized that there is a true challenge to let yourself to be as big as you can be and accepted by others. I started to see very clearly that this is not only my individual pain, but the pain of the whole human kind.

Therefore, in describing this pain, I use the pronoun 'we". It seems we willingly abuse ourselves because that is how we were taught. We manipulate and reduce ourselves in the name of others, although in reality it does not make those others happy. As a result, everyone suffers, believing that this is the only way to build relationships and life as a whole.

Especially because with each day it becomes scarier to let one's real self go—who knows what will jump out?! And we are rightfully afraid. In all this time, so much had accumulated of heavy feelings, pain, and suffering from the actual process of squeezing the spring that it seems that it would be better not to open this Pandora's box at all. So, we end up with a repetitious cycle. We try to be convenient, nice, comfortable, and unintimidating, thus depriving ourselves and others of the natural right of being themselves. Becoming a parent and continuing this our supposedly noble choice of sacrifice, we take this right away from our most loved ones, from our children. Thus, we pass this heavy "noble" burden from generation to generation. But what is the point—is it possible to break this debilitating sequence?

My realization of this journey to ultimate inner freedom of being as big as I can be, began with admitting that feeling of a clenched spring. It happened when, inside I felt that I could do much more and even the people around say that I have great potential, but for some reason all that potential remained buried deep inside or in my imagination. There I was a free and creative person, who is not afraid to express herself. In other words, there, in my imagination, all my nature is full of colors and life, but what projects outside is some pitiful imitation of that picture. Individual streaks, completely unrelated to each other, not whole, deprived of meaning and life. So, the picture ends up being neither truthful, nor complete. But it is acceptable, suitable for the common standard.

And again, it is possible to tell one's self, having listened to the people around say clever things, that one should be content with little and be grateful for what one has at the end of the day. I agree when it is about objects, meaningless material items. But I could not feel grateful for what I was on the outside, knowing how big I felt myself inside. I felt this kind of gratitude to be fake. I did not want to be content with what was left of me after the years of squeezing myself. Feeling I was betraying myself, I knew that somewhere inside my Inner Home there are hidden treasures, and important and valuable parts of my personality. Yet no one sees them but me. And the more I hide them and pretend that everything is right, the more they become heavy and offensive. It is not that the opinion or the judgment of the others is important to me, or that they see all of me. It is my own awareness of this big wonderful living space within me that was taken from me, that I desperately needed to come back to, releasing myself from the inner burdens and sharing it with the world.

So, this big space, unexplored by me, that I was hiding in my fantasies, always attracted me. With time, I began to pay attention and listen to this faraway, quiet voice that came from a mysterious inner space. It almost whispered into my ear, at times even secretly, "You are more; you can do much more; you are wider and brighter than it seems. You are more multifaceted and profound." I think that it was precisely this inner voice—the one that knew the truth about me and seemed to be what I sometimes thought to be nonsense, a fantasy, or a dream—this voice pushed me ahead toward my own Inner Home, toward the feeling that I am finally moving freely along the entire inner space, opening the right doors, finding new rooms, exploring new territories and inhabiting them.

And so, I transformed this voice into action. Not really knowing what I was doing, I felt a strong need to act, to create any movement toward this new, big space. This action became the move from Russia to Israel, when at the age of sixteen, I literally set out to conquer new territories. This was my first step toward freedom, toward something bigger than what I knew about myself. Often, when changing the place, space, or finding ourselves in some new circumstances, it is as if we receive a second chance to start everything anew. Questions arose, sometimes a little fearfully: What if this time I will not clamp up, what if I manage to escape from my own prison, and finally become big and free?

Having this independence in Israel and taking care of myself, I could feel that the inner string opens up slowly, not easily, and the excitement from the first sip of freedom faded after a while. And so began the work: Immersing into myself and sorting the endless mountain of trash accumulated over the years; freeing my inner space and broadening of my own boundaries, step by step. I began a journey toward my potential

Home, toward something bigger, something beyond the line, beyond the boundary of what I knew about myself, but what I so often imagined and what I so desperately believed. I had begun my journey toward something bigger than who I was that day.

This space, bigger than I am, still attracts me today. It beckons me and helps me to accomplish the most passionate, thrilling and most daring things on the way to my own potential. It is no longer possible to stop this force inside me; it takes increasingly more space in my inner universe. But it is only now, after a long and exhausting struggle, that I am not fighting for or capturing anything anymore, but, in my own body, am just moving toward it more freely. This does not mean that the journey is always smooth, but it is not a war any longer. As I move toward my potential, this space it occupies is always—even if just by a little— bigger than me. Using my soul navigator that takes me down the freest, most natural, and safe way, I move patiently overcoming my own barriers, walls, and boundaries, and feeling great happiness and a true gratitude on this journey.

A message from my Inner Personal Assistant who helps me recognize my inner strengths and powers:

You have learned to believe that you are always more than you think and that trusting and following this force will inevitably carry you over your walls, barriers, and boundaries, and will gradually open you to your real true self—cosmic and endless. You see clearly that you have an entire life for this, so need not be in a rush, but simply continue to walk and believe in your journey. You learned to trust that there is always a greater space that awaits you ahead. You know when you are ready to open to this space and accept it as a part of your large size. With every step, your Inner Home become wider, bigger, and more profound.

The Next Steps:
Creating a Safe Container
and Structure

No matter what your destination is right now,
you are always on The Way Home.

On the Way to
My Inner Personal Space

I grew up without knowing what personal space was. In the Russian language—the language of my childhood—there is not even such definition, it is merely a translation from English. In that culture and mentality such a concept did not exist. I am not talking here about personal physical space. In the time when I was a child, many kids already had their own rooms, and so did I. That is, I had my personal physical space and I appreciated it. But even so, that space could not substitute or replace the psychological, emotional, energetic personal space—the natural, safe space for my soul.

I see this safe space as a place where I am free to express my thoughts, feelings, emotions, reactions, choices and inner movements. It is the kind of space where I can allow myself to vent everything that is warmed up and ready to be aired at that moment, no matter its value or significance. It does not matter whether this self-expression is constructive and creative, an intermediate stage of something unformed and unclear, or simply will pass in a moment. The space that I dreamed of is the possibility of a free, unfiltered expression of my inner world, my inner nature, even if it may bring me some difficulties, painful experience, or discomfort. In my imagination, it is this neutral space, or container, where any colors, communications, inner movements may appear on the walls at any time. This space does not have to correspond to any external parameters and criteria, it does not have to be subjected to any evaluations or analyses. It is simply my personal safe neutral space, my inner free territory, where I can be the way I am at any moment and express myself freely and naturally. In this space, I do not need to justify myself to anyone, explain anything, or care about how it will be understood and accepted—because this is my unique and creative personal space, here I can be the way I want to be.

So, even as an adult, the question arose for me: How can I allow myself to wish and search for this wonderful space? And most importantly, can I assume the responsibility for the creation of such a safe, free and natural container for my soul that is my own personal inner territory?

First, I had to calm down one persistent voice in my own head. I had heard these thoughts tens of times, especially from the older generation. They all united into one solid, strong voice that kept convincing me that my very request, my need for this inner personal space is illegitimate, and hence does not merit even the wish to create it. This voice sounded somewhat like this: "Somehow we managed to live without this inner personal space, this inner freedom. We lived in difficult conditions, our parents paid no attention to us whatsoever, nobody bothered to respect us. Yet, nothing happened, we survived, and keep surviving without asking for more. You, on the other hand, don't even know what else to come up with, nothing is enough for you. So, now you need to have rights for this inner space too..." And so forth. This loud, collective voice is trying to assure me that what I am looking for is not real, it makes no sense, is egotistical, and contradicts many norms and canons of our society. Maybe it is even chaotic and dangerous.

Now, after many years of self-doubts, confusion and fears, I shall respond to this voice that is stuck in my head so deeply. Everything around me is constantly moving and evolving, and I am no longer surprised at the speed with which our world is changing. So, why should my inner world exist under the laws dictated by the reality of years past? Why, inside me, do I have to settle for the norms that, perhaps, were life-saving at one point, but are no longer relevant for me today? In the past, especially in my country, Russia, the ability to be silent, hush up, clam up, endure, and survive was vitally important. People could not afford a different way of living. This ability to be silent and hide inner processes, even from themselves, often simply saved people's lives. Very few dared to even dream about discovering and freely expressing their inner world. Those who tried to find such a space inside them often succumbed to the power of drugs, alcohol, fanaticism, or a disconnect from reality. This happened because they had finally felt this freedom of expression as a gasp of fresh air after being locked away, and, perhaps, they were unable to exist in that dangerous border where freedom ends and chaos begins.

But times change, and so does my inner world, my needs and my own rights. Today, being able to express myself freely and naturally is not just 'nice to have' anymore. It is a true and justified necessity. It is a well-deserved right for my own safe, free space of a natural and true self-expression; a space for trials and errors, release of emotions, expression of my incomplete ideas and creations, fears, confusions and pain from the very process of growth.

In my inner personal container, I want to give freedom to everything that needs to be expressed, even if it is not yet ready to be outside my Inner Home, not ready to be publicly shared yet. For all that goes on within me, I need a space that is private and contained, as if detached from the outside world. There is nothing selfish or egotistical in this. On the contrary, it is a responsibility for my inner nature—a responsibility for what I bring to this outside world and how I manifest myself in it. This issue of responsibility can be seen two ways: I express myself in a contained and adequate way, after I have had some time in my personal inner space to let myself be as true and free as I needed; or I suppress and hide my inner nature, even in my own inner world, and don't take any responsibility of what is getting outside by mistake.

Working and communicating with many different people, I noticed that today many of us are caught between two extreme edges. On the one hand, we can choose to live while clamping everything up inside, constantly restricting and forcing ourselves to be normal. Or, we can run away, renounce, distance ourselves from this world and reality in order to finally be true and free, to finally have this safe and free personal space for our soul. But, I truly believe that we all deserve better than that. That each of us has a right and responsibility to create this internal personal space-container that will be safe and free. Each of us needs this inner freedom and ownership of his/her inner world. Because only then we will be able to share our truth with each other and feel at Home with who we are.

Today I choose gradually to accustom myself to this free, natural, creative and safe inner container. Day by day, it becomes a part of my routine, my natural reality, and my life. I slowly learn to live in it. In this space, I can fall from one extreme into another, eventually finding the golden middle. I can cross my inner boundaries to know for certain where they are and respect them deliberately, and not because I was taught to or scared into doing so. In this space, I do foolish things to fully appreciate my true wisdom. I make mistakes to learn to trust my intuition and my instincts. I let myself be distracted or do nothing at all to determine what is really important to me. In my inner personal space, I am allowed all of this. There, I will not lie, hide, run away, destroy, suffer from loneliness, withdraw, or take my own life. Because, this is my safe space where I am held and supported by my unique inner container. I can let my inner nature express itself freely, because this nature is wise and beautiful, even in its darkest moments. I can be different, distinct, not always coinciding with other kinds of nature, because that is the way my life becomes truly full and expressive, becomes a part of greater Creation.

My Inner Heart Companion shares her thoughts:

I love my inner personal space, in which my Inner Home is protected and can be expanded. My inner contained territory is not an obstacle to the others, but rather a thread that connects me to everything living, natural and free. I do not need this space to be visible or noticeable from the outside; I only need to allow myself to have this personal inner container where I can express my real self in the form in which I am today, here-and-now. Because only through containing and expressing my true self today, can I fully feel at Home with myself.

On the Way through Fears to Being Safe

I had no idea how terrified I was... Well, of course, not all of me, just some of my parts. My Inner Home is full of different rooms, tones, individual qualities and forces. But when I started to settle and explore my Inner Home, I discovered a dark scary space (I imagine it as a closet) that was still full of fears and dark shadows. When I enter this dark corner, everything inside freezes—and, therefore, everything is terrifying. All the remaining rooms, lights, and colors are immediately forgotten, and I only remember that heart chilling terror, as if it is the only me, as if it is the master. Like a horror movie, this feeling reminded me of a scene from the movie *Sixth Sense*, when only the protagonist of the film, the boy, saw the dead people around him.

Opening this inner closet, you can also see things, or even experience things that nobody else can see from the outside. The people around cannot see and feel these things because these fears are inside and real for you only. When this inner closet is touched, even casually, all of your scariest feelings and memories pour out. And you might feel yourself at that moment precisely at the age when you initially went through those terrifying experiences. You are no longer a smart, grown up, and multifaceted person, but a terrified child who does not understand how he can escape from this horror movie, and whether he can be rescued at all.

So, the question arises: Is it possible to feel truly safe again in one's own Inner Home? When we step out of the safety of our physical home, our survival instincts help and protect us. In such situations, fear becomes a natural signal that helps us recognize danger. But, when alone with ourselves, what are we afraid of in our own Inner Home, a place that should be our bastion?

Unfortunately, or fortunately, the scariest beasts, killers, tyrants, skeletons, and dragons are inside us, hiding in those dark corners of our inner world, and waiting for the moment to jump at us like a jack-in-the-box and paralyze us with fear. When these hidden issues appear, there are people who try to get rid of them in a practical way: Pull on the protective gloves (this is a good option), pick up a can of poison spray, axe, sword, or other weapons, and take the enemy out! Without any sentiment or worries, we just cut this rubbish out and start living freely, breathing deeply, in this clean and safe home. It sounds attractive and a viable option for those bugs. But with time, I realized that living through those internal monsters does not work quite so simply.

Let us say, you became tired of being scared and decided it was time to face your fears, usually a good and healthy decision. And so, you put on your armor, choose your weapon and amulets, and pray before your journey. You step out, brave and courageous, to fight your monster, perhaps hidden in a closet somewhere in a dark corner, or in a box in the attic. You take a deep breath, steady your weapon, open the door, and...suddenly, in that remote place, together with all the skeletons, monsters, and other horrors, you see a terrified and trembling little girl (or boy) who sits curled into a ball, shaking with fear. Are you going to get rid of her too? She is a live being, a part of you. And that is when you realize that the scariest and the most terrifying things here are not the skeletons, dragons, et al., but this tiny horrified, with eyes-full-of-fear, child. She or he had been sitting in that closet, God only knows for how long, in complete darkness with all those monsters around, and no one, not a single person to come to his or her rescue. And then you squat in front of this child and extend your arms to him or her, because only you can protect this child—and you both know it. The child now begins to move slowly, stretch its little numb hands, and reaches out to you. And later, when you both will be sitting under a blanket to get warm and away from soul-chilling cold and drinking tea, that child will tell you all his scariest stories—talking non-stop, laughing and crying. And you will laugh and cry because you will feel sorry for that child, but also, simultaneously, you will feel relieved that you two have finally met. This part of re-connection lasts for a while—for as long as it takes.

And then, in a little while, together you will collect all those skeletons, dragons, and monsters (pain, mourning, loneliness, grief) and put them back into the box. Because they will no longer be alive—they will be merely symbols, parts of your story. Yes, maybe they will be unpleasant, sad, or even disgusting, but they will not scare and terrify anymore because the one who was afraid is now warm, heard, and no longer alone. And that means there is no one for her to be afraid of. You will put that box into the closet, close the door, and open the curtains in the room so that the natural light will come in and illuminate every corner. The room will be much brighter; you will look at it, hugging the child, and think that it is not so scary and with a little bit of light and color you can even live there, or at least spend some time in it, feeling safe.

It sounds very simple but it is so hard to find this little inner child and bring safety into his/her life. How many times do we find ourselves in denial of our inner child's fears? How many times do we choose to turn back and not hear his or her cry for help, instead trying to find an 'adult' solution to the problem? The one used most often is explanation or rationalization, telling the child there's nothing to be afraid of. Just as, when only seeing the outline of those ominous skeletons, we tell ourselves: "So what? This is not even a skeleton, just a few bones, nothing to fear. Look at other people, they have gone through real horrors, and yet they survived, they live and are not afraid. And mine is only a small monster, a tiny dragon. I'm even embarrassed to talk about it." Each time we say this to ourselves we leave our scared inner child all alone with his/her fears. We try to convince ourselves that we are no longer afraid, but that child knows the truth. He or she is still very scared and lonely. He or she waits for us and hopes that we will come to his/her rescue, no matter how ridiculous his/her fears may seem to us today.

In our Inner Home, there are many such corners and closets, full of hidden fears, some scarier than others. But, as I was opening those deeply hidden closets, cabinets, and boxes, I made the realization that it is impossible to compare, measure, or estimate the inner weight of these fears until you get to that child who sits there and hear him out completely, with attention and sincere empathy. Returning to the protagonist of "The Sixth Sense": the only thing that helped him overcome all his fears was the fact that he was not alone. There was an adult by his side who believed that this child was scared, listened to him, and empathized with him. That adult sometimes was scared just as the boy was, but he never left the boy alone. And, inside each of us there exists such an adult who can and should set out in search of those lost little children. Supporting my clients on this journey, I have learned to take, instead of weapons, a warm blanket and a stuffed toy from childhood, which can be a lot more reassuring to the child than a weapon.

On my own personal journey, I had never suspected that I was so frightened until I had begun looking for my lost childhood parts. There are many examples of all the fears, big and little, that I found and those that are still hidden away somewhere in my inner closet, awaiting their turn. Some have recognizable names: fear of rejection, fear of being as big I want to be, fear of the unknown, fear of losing control. Others are more amorphous such as fear of my vulnerability, fear of my powers, fear of being myself. Others seem to stem from childhood: fear of being not good enough, fear of making mistakes, fear of not doing it right. Monsters are there, too, and they have recognizable names: the powerful dragons of shame and blame; horrifying creatures such as abuse, self-destruction, and deep loneliness.

Yet, it is more important to tell about my long-lost inner children that I found. These children are now safe, because in my today's Inner Home I care about them and their safety, I listen to them, hug them, warm them up, and calm them down. They will forever remain children who went through trauma alone and thus will always need my attention and care. But from the moment they were freed, they have continued to grow with me and with each day are becoming stronger and braver. And so am I. With each day, too the feeling of safety in my Inner Home is clearer. And since my Inner Home is always with me—no matter where or with whom I am—that feeling of safety spreads far beyond my physical home because inside it is safe, warm, peaceful and not lonely. The comfort and safety I feel, also spread to those with whom I am in contact, sometimes without my knowledge. This is a special gift.

My Inner Heart Companion has a message here for all inner children:

A little frightened inner child, so brave, so wonderful, so tireless. It is so hard to fight all fears alone. Sometimes you feel so tired, so cold, so weak. How you want to simply cover up with a warm blanket, curl up in a ball, fall asleep, and see peaceful, colorful dreams. How you want someone kind and wise to stroke your little head and say that everything is going to be okay. How you long for others to trust you, to believe in your fears without demanding any proof—to just look into your wide-open, full-of-fear eyes. How you yearn for someone to turn on the light and sweep away the darkness.

You are absolutely right, little one, that you deserve all this. You will find that if you do not despair, do not freeze completely, and do not fall asleep forever, even if you scream, cry, call for help, get angry, fight for your life, that you will find safety. You will find this because you deserve to live, feeling safe. Sooner or later you will be found, no matter how far or deep you are hiding from the fear. You will be found by that kind and wise adult for whom you are waiting so anxiously.

You will ask me of these times, "Was I on the way Home?" And I will answer, "Of course, because all the roads lead to Home. Especially, when you let your heart lead you."

On the Way to Being
My Own Appropriate Authority

While styles of raising children change over time and cultures, living and working in different countries, I notice that many children are being taught not only to obey and respect their elders but also take everything the adults say as the only possible and absolutely unassailable truth. Regardless of the cultural background, many kids are growing up in belief that their parents 'know what's best for them'. And the parents sometimes spend years on training their children to accept and follow similar rules and laws.

Here is the interesting part: I have only met a few who would assume the responsibility to undo these orders when the time comes. That is, when an adult can tell his child, "Now you are responsible for yourself and only you know what is best for you. Only you can allow or forbid yourself something. Only your decision regarding your life has value, and you have the last word, because now you are your own authority. Respect your inner voice and trust it, the same way you trusted me." Unfortunately, such conversations take place very rarely. Even if they did take place, most of us still remain deeply infantile, insecure in ourselves, and unable to take responsibility for our actions and decisions, even as adults.

Many people do not even realize that they still live according to someone else's orders, rules and decisions, without allowing themselves to think with their own head and be guided by their own intuition and life experience. Even if some are able to recognize that the time has come for them to become their own authority, often times they simply do not know how to do it, because all their life they had been followers. Or, perhaps, they were under the oppression of an authority that they want to forget as soon as possible and avoid taking any responsibilities at all. Sometimes, people who were led for so many years, become the same uncompromising authority for their own children—supposedly knowing what is best, and yet not having any idea about their own lives and not taking responsibility for themselves. And, so the cycle repeats from generation to generation.

The above posits a question: How is it possible to work up the courage to become my own authority, my own author? Not just any authority, but an appropriate one that corresponds to me, to my Inner Voice, my Inner Home?

For my own story, I was very lucky that my parents, ever since I was very little, gave me a chance to make my own decisions and choices and to take responsibility for my actions. Thanks to them I matured early and became very independent and responsible for my entire life. But this was only true externally, in my inner life I didn't have any authority whatsoever.

On the inside, I was full of doubts about myself, my own feelings and thoughts. It always seemed to me that there is someone else who knows what is best for me; that my own feelings were less important or true, that my view and ideas about life had a much lesser value than those of someone else. The problem was not that I was insecure of myself because I was young and inexperienced, and it was not that around me there were many people who were smarter, more experienced, and with more authority. It was that I rejected my own self. I simply did not trust my inner life. I did not believe that my feelings were right, that my ideas worth sharing, that I knew what was true for me.

I was not used to the idea that only I was responsible for my inner world; that it was my right to handle my own thoughts and feelings however I wanted; that I could think, feel, see, hear, experience, and express anything and everything I wanted. I did not know that my inner world was my personal territory, and no one had the right to land on it without my permission. Most of all, I was hesitant to accept that only I knew what kind of authority suited me, and that only I could be such authority for myself.

Of course, it was very hard to trust myself right away. I needed proof. So, I put all my effort into proving to myself that I can be trusted, that I am worthy of this high title "authority". I needed to earn this authority in my own eyes. Luckily, life was presenting many and varied situations and circumstances where I could prove to myself and grow into my own perception.

Pertaining to finding my authority, I believe I was very lucky that my first child, my son, was born when I was only 21 years old, and my daughter was born when I was 24. I was lucky, not only because they came into my life and filled it with a new and special meaning and significance, but also because they gave me an opportunity to see what I was capable of. I could show myself what kind of parent I could be and, respectively, what kind of authority I would be for myself. It was precisely because of this inner desire to become a good enough mother for myself, that was constantly growing, and continues to grow, in the role of a mother. Through trial and error, through bold questions and sincere answers, I was proving to myself that I deserved to be trusted, that I can take myself seriously. I was proving to myself that my thoughts, my instincts, my intuition, and my inner reactions have a positive effect. Paying attention to my entire inner world brought benefit for my children. I was able to make them happy by creating a calm, warm and safe home atmosphere.

Gradually, in an empirical way, I put together for myself my own settings and values that were not created by someone or heard somewhere else, but came from my life, sincere and honest. For example, it was important for me to not only show respect and trust toward my children's actions and decisions, but, most importantly, towards their inner territory. It was much more important for me that my children could hear the voice of their own inner authority than consider me as such. Since they were very little, I consistently replied to them: "I don't know what's best for you. Only you can know it. I can give you advice, tell you what I would do, but the decision is ultimately yours."

So, it is not surprising that my children, who are now teenagers, know very well what they need and what they want. It is not always the most convenient point of view for us, the parents. But when it comes to some sort of peer pressure that so often occurs at this age, the chance that they will give into something they do not want to do or feel is not right, is minimal. My twelve-year-old girl says, "It doesn't feel right." For her, this is a powerful enough argument to not do or participate in something. I truly believed that it was their job to understand and get to know themselves (through trial and error) and gradually become an appropriate authority for themselves. My role is guide and to share my experience, especially the one that I have already processed with myself. Most interesting is that it is precisely this approach that created a deep respectful bond among us. It is as if by relieving my children from my authority, I gave them a chance to show respect to me on their own accord, and not as part of some forced agreement.

I think this early parenting experience helped me realize that the only way to feel my own authority is to understand what type actually suits me. Just as each child has his own individual needs, and each child (even within one family) needs his own kind of parent, I, initially, had to figure out what kind of inner parent I needed for myself. I had to learn my true needs, the ones that were satisfied and especially the ones that were not. I had to create an image of an inner grown-up—the one I wanted to obey and whom I wanted to become. I needed to assure my inner child (mind you, convince him with actions, not with words) that I hear him/her and see what he/she needs. I did not merely play a role of a 'good parent' for myself; instead, I sincerely tried to respect everything that happened within me and assumed full responsibility for it. Only then was I able to finally feel my own inner appropriate authority. I believe, that by assuming this internal role, I will never step onto someone else's inner territory because he who is truly his own authority has no need to infringe on something that is not his. He who is truly responsible for his Inner Home, will not take advantage or take hostage of someone else's Inner Home.

The message my Inner Heart Companion speaks:

I imagine my inner authority to be my feminine beginning. It treats me with great warmth, care, and trust. It can be strict and just. It is not afraid to tell me the truth about myself because sincerity and honesty are more important to it than pleasantness and comfort of interaction. It trusts in me, in my endeavors, expressions, ideas, and dreams. It hears me and is willing to change together with me. It gives me the right to err and supports me in difficult times. Most importantly, it gives me a chance to be myself, and not someone else. It insists that I remain faithful and loyal to my truth, my nature, my soul. It is a part of me— the very part that is ready to take the responsibility, to be an honest, confident, and caring hostess of my Inner Home: the keeper of my inner hearth.

The Journey of Clarity
and Action

No matter what your destination is right now,
you are always on The Way Home.

On the Way between
Action and Inaction

As a child, I was always taught the importance of staying busy. The entire country where I grew up was saturated with such postulates as: "A man is judged by his actions."; "He who does not work does not eat.", and "Business before pleasure.", etc. In the Soviet Union, there existed a specific term, *tuneyadets* (in English the closest would be *parasite*) for a person who was not officially employed anywhere. Moreover, there was even a legal statute permitting incarceration of such an individual. Many artists, poets, and other people of creative professions who were not officially enrolled in any employment organization ended up locked away during those years. Among those of my parents', and especially my grandparents', generation, a person was valued for his deeds. People were busy from dawn to dusk with various tasks, and one of the main and most important metrics was the opportunity to see specific results of one's work. The more productivity the person brought, the more valued one was by those others.

Those were very complicated times that dictated their own laws. As a consequence, acting in a way that would allow one to survive, advance, break through, move in the direction towards a better life was really necessary. Those generations tended to act, and not talk. Even though I was born at the end of that epoch, in my family action was always praised, while inaction was looked down upon. For example, I remember very clearly that as a child, I was not permitted to simply lie on the sofa. Of course, nobody was standing over me at every instant, but when my mother saw me lying on the sofa, she would say something unpleasant or make a face that made me jump right up. I remember the feeling of guilt when someone would catch me 'not doing anything'. As a response to that, I occasionally would fabricate some sickness because then one can lie on the sofa and do absolutely nothing. Often, I would try to cause or 'awaken' the sickness in me, just to be able to enjoy the pleasure of doing nothing. Those were happy times.

Many years had passed before I realized my true motive and allowed myself to, in fact, do nothing—without getting sick, and thus freeing myself from the endless colds, unknown viruses, and an overall weakness. As soon as I allowed myself to do nothing without a sufficient reason, my poor health practically stopped bothering me, as I no longer had a need for it.

In the process of growing up, my attitude toward being in constant action went through many changes. As noted, on the one hand, a very strong childish desire to allow myself to do nothing resided inside me—at least when no one was watching. But the guilty feeling that accompanied this would spoil all the joy and fun. It was impossible to get rid of that voice in my head that lectured me for having wasted time and for utter laziness. So, I kept hiding from my inner voice, trying to convince it that I absolutely must lie down at that moment because I was very weak, or I could not complete some task because I was incapable of doing it. I even begged myself for a vacation, hiding behind a series of seemingly important excuses, inventing stories, just to have that precious opportunity to do nothing without being punished for it. Yet, when I was in action, I most often was extremely productive. That is, my eagerness and energy sometimes would perform miracles in achieving objectives and goals. Looking back, I sometimes see myself as a wound-up toy that ran at a crazy speed until I ran out of power or the motor would turn off, and then I would fall down, completely disconnected. It appears that neither in action nor inaction was I free and true to myself; I was following some external laws, habits, and definitions imposed on me.

At some point, I believe when I was about twenty-two years-old, I heard that there is a concept called a "state of being", that is, when one's presence and inner perception is not defined by actions or results. It is when one can simply "be". Suddenly, an entire new world opened to me—the world that would support and inspire you in the process of just "being". In my understanding the state of "being" was juxtaposed with that of "doing". In other words, one is either in the process of being and lives every instant of his life, or he chooses action and works for a result, achieving external targets, but at the same time losing the connection with himself and the present moment. During that period of my life, that juxtaposition was very convenient for me. Now I had finally found a perfect reason for doing nothing, encompassing wise, and philosophical ideas that, indeed, contained truth (unlike my previous implausible excuses).

So, with a clear conscience I submerged myself in the state of "being". Of course, it was wonderful. My constant desire to think, to dream, to go into myself finally was realized. I began to allow myself to simply "float in space", not making any plans for the future, but rather living through feelings and perceptions instead of actions. At that moment, I had begun to explore various spiritual practices, meditated, developed an interest in metaphysics, the power of energy. Most importantly, I had begun to listen very closely to my inner world. It was a pivotal period of my life that helped me start my journey Home, to my real and true self.

Nevertheless, even by holding onto the feeling of "being" and praising it, I still was not able to reach the desired equilibrium. Essentially, I could not truly get to know myself. It is possible to spend a long period of time to think about what I am like; imagine, dream, analyze, evaluate, and define. But only in action is it possible to feel ourselves and receive precious life experience that is incomparable in its value to any ideas we might have about ourselves, however profound and wise they might be. The experience remains within us on many levels—physical, mental, and emotional alike. It is what becomes our essential substance.

Later, when exploring the theory of psychodrama as a therapeutic method, I was surprised at the healing force that action and action methods play for us. The core principle of psychodrama is not directed at discussing, describing, talking about, or analyzing something; rather, it is about showing, feeling, and experiencing. I continue to be amazed by the kind of transformations that can happen with someone when, for example, he does not talk about his fear, but rather assumes the role of his own fear and speaks in the first person; or when someone does not talk about a conflict with his father, but rather conducts a dialogue with him, becoming first himself and then his father. This allows 'the protagonist' (as one is called in psychodrama) to not only comprehend the depth of one's own processes, but also the point of view of the other person, and sometimes, the dynamics of their relationship. I have found the use of psychodramatic methods to be invaluable also when I am working with children. I often offer them instead of telling me about their dream—for example, becoming a star singer—an opportunity to show me, to assume the role and live a few moments of that performance that was born in their imagination. After such an experience, I have often felt that the child would suddenly and truly come alive; that he would awaken into life and express himself on the outside in a much more confident and courageous way, as if relying on that experience.

After I discovered for myself the beauty and depth of inaction, and the power and importance of action, a new and very interesting period began for me—and still continues to this day. First, I started to feel enormous joy from both states. Instead of juxtaposing them, I allowed them to walk hand-in-hand. Often times, they would even morph into one whole, and then I could manage to enjoy inaction amidst a very rapid action. It is as if I were building a bridge between my inner and external realities; between a thin and transparent substance and a concrete one; between images and metaphors and clear and understood actions that bring those images to life. I would give my inner movements an opportunity to transform into an external action. Sometimes, I may appear inactive on the surface, while feeling all the activity that takes place within. Sometimes, I privately enjoy the inner silence while happily participating in external activities. And, of course, I am learning to comprehend myself—both in action and inaction, both in "being" and "doing". It is thus that I connect My Inner Home with the world around me.

This message from my Inner Personal Assistant, who recognizes my inner strengths and resources, further clarifies this issue between being and doing:

Your strength is in keeping the balance between these two states, in holding them both. When you are able to accept yourself in action and in inaction, you can enjoy the "middle", the space that between them. When you release yourself from all the beliefs about these two states and just observe yourself, you are able to be both. Then your Inner Home can be very active, while your life is easy and relaxed. Your Inner Home can be also quite and comforting, while you go through a lot of activities, achievements and outside results.

On the Way to
Clarity and Cleanliness

"It is a question of discipline, when you've finished washing and dressing each morning, you must tend to your planet."
    The Little Prince, Antoine de Saint Exupery

I would imagine that everyone appreciates when their home is clean and orderly. Of course, I am not referring to a synthetic cleanliness, akin to a hospital. I am talking about cleanliness as care, beauty, culture, something natural and alive that helps us move through life easily and freely. Cleanliness conveys a feeling of clarity, tranquility, lightness, and concentration at the same time, even health. But cleanliness requires work, for which we often do not have the energy or sometimes even the desire. And the dirtier and more cluttered our home, the harder it can be to start cleaning. Sometimes, the task of even beginning seems unbearable, and we may continue to live in a cluttered space and unknowingly be stifled from lack of clean air.

For many people I have met, the cleaning of the physical home may be associated with punishment, humiliation, or sometimes having been required to keep it almost antiseptically clean. Therefore, the process of cleaning very often becomes not only a physical, but a psychological challenge to overcome,

120

for which we need enormous effort. But what is even more grave or disturbing is when we do not care about the cleanliness and clarity of our Inner Home. The danger here lies in the fact that we do not see—and sometimes do not even recognize—our own clutter and inner mess. Furthermore, to many of us it seems as if this trash is not visible to others, and if it is not visible and does not smell, why clean at all? Most importantly, no one can really persuade us to clean our inner space. If in our physical home we can hear pleas or reproaches from our family, friends, or people coming into our house—in the Inner Home, everyone is really his own boss. And no matter what others say, we can always reply, "This is my personal business, I live the way I want to."

So, it turns out that our inner cleanliness and clarity is truly our own responsibility. This is each person's personal choice based on an inner ethical code. Unfortunately, not only we ourselves, but also those around us, suffer from all our accumulated inner mess, including unnecessary thoughts, hard feelings, unprocessed traumas and destructions, and emotions that were not expressed appropriately or in a timely manner. We experience all that weight inside and, consciously or subconsciously, might feel a need to throw out some of that heavy trash. It seems, that if we can release something, we will feel more at ease. *(I am not speaking here about the state in which we are looking for support and empathy. In that situation, we can ask for help or share what hurts or bothers us, not expecting that person to heal us or make our pain go away; rather, we simply hope that this person will listen to us and offer empathy, and we will feel relieved and cleansed.)* But, there are those moments when we spill out what we can no longer keep inside onto those close to us, without asking whether they want, or are ready, to accept it. We simply throw our trash onto someone else. Most times, those portions of trash land on those whom we trust the most, who, we are sure, will not stop loving us, will not turn or run away from us. And, these situations are mostly unconscious because our Inner Home is clouded and crowded.

Such life examples are everywhere, well beyond the more trivial, everyday trash-throwing onto each other, when people release their anger, frustration and stress. There are much more complicated cases of projecting the inner mess onto someone else. For example, a mother, feeling herself unaccomplished, begins to pressure her child, convincing him that he is not fully using his potential. A husband who is losing interest in life, reproaches his wife for being boring and not interested in anything. A young man who suffers from low self-esteem, blames the friend for preferring other friends over him. A father, feeling his own helplessness, constantly sees his son as weak and does everything to make the son believe so as well. The list goes on. The dangerous thing in such situations is that one does not even realize what he is doing. To him, it may seem that he is sharing his knowledge, experience, or reality. In some way, he *does* share his inner reality, inner life—a life that has become one big mess and needs to be cleared. Unfortunately, this throwing out of trash becomes a destructive recycling, when the second person takes it all personally, retains it in his own baggage, and clutters his own inner space. The danger expands when he then casts out his garbage onto someone else. And, so, the cycle continues and we question how to break it. How are we to learn to sustain our inner cleanliness and clarity? How do we turn inner cleaning into an everyday, natural personal hygiene?

On the way to defining and living my own personal hygiene, I have found the journey to have several qualifications and cautions. Sometimes, a very fastidious or cautious person can mistake inner hygiene and cleanliness with the desire not 'to mess' him or herself in the first place. In other words, they may maintain an artificial or fake cleanliness—trying not to think of anything bad, repressing feelings, avoiding a relationship, closing their heart, not taking risks, never indulging in sweets, not moving from one spot. In their attempts at utter cleanliness, they are not really living; they are not alive.

Other variations on cleaning are that some people clean on auto-pilot, on a pre-set day without any concentrated thought or determination. An example of such automatic inner cleaning may be a weekly trip to a psychologist or to a Sunday Mass or religious service. They will 'get cleaned' once a week and continue on their way. This type of cleaning is surface cleaning and, while good for general maintenance, will not make much difference in clearing a path to inner knowledge and wellness.

For me, inner cleanliness is the clarity of thought, purity of vision, light and clean energy, an open heart, a sense of safety and freedom, and feelings of relaxation and concentration in my body. Loving cleanliness and clarity, I make it so that around and inside me there would be clean space—not blurred and cluttered with unnecessary objects that distract my attention. To maintain my daily hygiene, I need to see and notice what goes on around and inside me on a continual basis. Being clear for me is when I can live, without fear of messing up, or being constantly ready to make an effort toward my own clarity of actions and thought. In other words, I can feel the joy of the actual process of cleaning as a natural process of life.

The main challenge that presented itself to me on my way to inner clarity was that I sometimes did not feel the connection with my Inner Home and, hence, did not have any motivation to do the cleaning. It was as if my mind, my psyche were saying, "What's the point of cleaning at this hotel when I'm only here temporarily? I don't feel like a host or an owner." To take this metaphor further, at a hotel, a person may feel like throwing everything around, not caring about the consequences. At some point, when the garbage seems or feels insurmountable, a person may even stop caring about it at all or defend him or herself with different mechanisms in order not to see, not to feel, not to smell, not to be connected to it. I, for example, was trying with all my strength to control the external order of my life, completely ignoring my inner world, which then became messy. Control of the external world was my defense mechanism and it blocked communication with my inner world.

That is how I realized that ownership of my Inner Home is the quality that was missing in those moments when I lacked motivation. And, ownership only happens when I take responsibility for my inner world, when I feel connected to it.

As with any process, the most important thing here is to begin—to take that first step, a different choice that can set a new way. I do not even remember anymore how my first major cleaning happened. But what matters is not how I did it, but that I made the actual decision and determination to get through all the trash, accumulated over the years, to my Inner Home, to my very true and natural self. That first cleaning took me a lot of time, and I believe this is the most meaningful and important work I have ever done in my life. I was convinced that once I would clear the path to myself, I would finally be able to relax and rest, enjoying the tranquility. But when I began to discover some parts of my true Inner Home, my everyday work on maintaining cleanliness and clarity in it had only begun. Now, this work has become joy and happiness for me and I am grateful for having something true and real to clean, to take care of, to keep clear and bright. This true sense of owning my Inner Home, my real home that I treasure is why keeping it clean is an important and valuable reward, instead of a debt or chore. I treat this work very responsibly and attentively because I realize that this is all I really have, and the better care I take of the cleanliness of my Inner Home, the nicer and cozier it will be to live in.

Yet, the job is not done; the journey is not over. I notice that each time when there is some disorder or mess (and it is impossible for it not to appear because I am an active person and live among active people), I begin to feel as though I am drifting away from myself. I stop caring about the life inside me, or want to turn away from the processes that take place in my Inner Home. Such feelings become the signals for me that a cleaning is in order. Or, sometimes, I get stuck in the outer reality, and on the inside unnecessary trash starts to accumulate. If I keep my senses and my awareness alive and in tune, I begin to notice an odor coming from that trash (and there is always an odor). At that point, I have learned to make myself stop and clean it up immediately, without postponing doing so. If I do it right away, it will not take much time, while my skills of inner cleaning improve with each day.

Nowadays, I accustom myself to a daily inner cleaning, just like little children learn to brush their teeth each day. I try to bring clarity to my inner space without throwing my inner trash onto others, brushing it under the rug, or covering it up with pretty things.

Many people today are aware of our home planet and exert much effort on cleaning the external space, the environment, nature. This is truly important. Similarly, it seems to me that if each person would take care of the cleanliness of their own nature, their Inner Home, many of today's problems, would diminish. As we all treat the cleanliness and clarity of our Inner Home with respect and attention, this care naturally expands to the world around us. Our entire planet, then, becomes our true home—a home where cleaning will not be a chore, but a natural expression of life.

My Inner Housekeeper relates to this topic very keenly and has the following message:

As you have learned, on this path toward cleanliness and clarity it is important to pay attention to what goes on in your Inner Home. It is precisely the attentiveness, sincere care, participation, respect toward your Inner Home that will help you determine when you need a Spring cleaning inside, and when it is enough to merely open the windows and air out your space; when inside you there is creative chaos, the type of chaos that clears itself up naturally, and when you need help from me, your Inner Housekeeper, who will assist you in sweeping out such destructive feelings like shame, blame, self-abuse.

Do not be afraid of dirt and trash; underneath them are hidden your most precious treasures, the cleanest and most natural parts of you. In your process of cleaning, many people around you may come out to help, support or participate. But most importantly, you can finally feel as a complete master and owner of your home. You can feel the responsibility and connection for your Inner Home. Truly love and cherish it. As you spend time and live in your clear, neat and cozy Inner Home, you will finally feel at home with yourself. That is a treasure worth working toward.

On the Way to
Inner Resilience

When I imagine the shape of my Inner Home, I see its edges or boundaries as flexible and resilient. These boundaries are firm and, at the same time, easily follow the movement within; they can change shape and expand. I greatly appreciate my inner ability to not get stuck in one place, not build inflexible structures, not remain petrified in an impulse to conserve a well-founded shape. This inner flexibility constantly pushes me toward new searches, changes, and growth that happens as a result of the process of inner movement. It also gives me an ability to react to unknown while believing that my inner shape will adjust to the external changes and sustain my Inner Home with its resilient and firm boundaries. I envision these boundaries as very strong and enduring, precisely because of their flexibility and elasticity.

Over the course of my life, just like any other person, I lived through many situations and life events. Not everything was easy, calm, or rosy. There were times that demanded resilience and the ability to recover quickly. Yet, I never focused on those external circumstances (or stories) that happened to me. I was always more interested in observing my own response to them, noticing what I discovered within myself as an answer to a particular external situation, sensing how exactly my inner world reacted to what was happening to me or my family. It does not mean that I closed in myself and dismissed solving the problems. I did what was necessary to overcome the circumstances or resolve a particular situation.

But my focus was always directed inward because it was more interesting and curious to me, the internal responses seeming more important and sincere than any life drama, as thrilling as it was. Sometimes I even did not wish to waste my energy on navigating through the drama that presented itself, simply because I could not take it seriously. Often, those external barriers appeared to me as fragments of some movie with which I simply could not connect. They appeared nothing more than some kind of a well-orchestrated and well-performed theatrical play. Even so, I was ready to notice the inner experience that those stories brought out in me, what they made *me* feel. On these feelings and experiences, I was more than willing to spend lots of energy, will, and persistence.

In the same way, it is always more interesting for me to learn about what another person feels inside, rather than only seeing the external situations he is going through. After speaking for hours on the phone, my best friend and I always laugh at the fact that we still never manage to ask each other what goes on in our lives—simply because we spend the entire time discussing our inner experiences, feelings, new expressions, difficulties, and discoveries. Each time when I finish my conversation with her, I happily realize how fulfilling and meaningful it was, and how much I learned about what actually is happening to her. I think that thanks to this ability of mine, helping my clients to navigate their inner world does not feel as a job to me, but rather as a natural and routine practice.

I realize that I have been very lucky in life as I so far have not faced a true tragedy or catastrophe—the loss of a loved one. I do not know how I would react in such a situation, how resilient I would be. Yet, if I were asked if I had ever experienced this, I would answer in the affirmative. This is because I know how loss, tragedy and grief feel, as if I went through these experiences as a part of my inner story. Because of this highly sensitive interior, I have always felt my inner story much more real, fuller, and deeper than circumstances that were happening to me. This is also why this book is not about what happened to me in life, but about what I discovered and collected within me, inside my Inner Home.

Looking back, I realize it was this intuitive focus that helped me show resilience and flexibility in the face of various life circumstances, changes, and surprises. Because of my inner energy, effort, and willingness to accept any inner movement or new piece of truth about myself, my inner boundaries grew stronger in flexibility and firmness. This inner elasticity and resilience are constantly working since my Inner Home is growing and expanding every day as new obstacles, barriers, and difficulties appear. Each day I also sense how this inner flexibility penetrates into my way of thinking, my logic, my reactions, how it influences my worldview, giving my Inner Home a possibility to remain a firm and resilient container where my soul can feel free, natural, and safe.

The message from my Inner Personal Assistant:

You have everything you need to feel safe and natural in your everyday life adventures. Your inner boundaries help you to be strong and allow you to be vulnerable, hence open and not guarded. Thanks to your inner flexibility and resilience, you can let your soul to be expressed and contained at the same time. You don't need to be on guard for your Inner Home because your inner boundaries are accurate enough to keep it safe. It gives you a chance to be curious, exploring and trusting, to follow the unfolding the truth. This did not happen in a day, you built these inner boundaries with a much patience and awareness. And as your Inner Personal Assistant I can say that it was mainly built on your intention to create a good-enough, strong, safe, flexible and natural Inner Home for your soul.

Corridors and Connectors

No matter what your destination is right now,
you are always on The Way Home.

On the Way from Independence
to
Co-dependence

When I was seven, I went to the first grade. I was sent to one of the best schools of the town, but it was fairly far from my home. I had to get from the house to the metro (about 10 minutes walking), ride the train for a couple of stops, and then walk from the station to the school (about 10-15 minutes walking). My mother told me that she was not going to be able to take me to and pick me up from school every day because her work was on the other side of the town. We had agreed that she would go with me for about two weeks, until I memorized the route, and then I would go and come back by myself. Now, when I am telling this, it seems unreasonable that a 7-year-old should be trusted, given that I took my ten-year-old daughter to school that is about 5 minutes from our home. Sometimes, when she wanted, she returned home by herself, but I tried to be free during that time to take her or pick her up from school. This is not because she needed me to do that, but because we both enjoyed the opportunity to walk together for a couple of minutes.

But back then, the times were different, both in the reality that surrounded me and the one inside me.

I remember that I was not scared at all of the decision to go by myself—on the contrary, I was very happy about it. I was so excited, as if a real adult life was finally beginning. I would belong only to myself, walk at the pace I wanted, look wherever I wanted, think about whatever I wanted, and enjoy my own company. The last days that my mother went with me I even asked her to follow a bit further behind, as if I were already going to school by myself. On these days, I would look at people's faces, and it seemed that they all were looking at me with admiration. They would look and think, "Wow, such a little girl, and yet she is already riding the metro by herself. She is such an independent and mature girl." And I walked, very proud of myself, with a sense that I did not need anybody, I could be by myself. Those were the good days.

And so came my first day of an independent life. I don't remember that very day itself, but I do recall many that followed it, and not all were the 'good days'. I remember waking up to the alarm early in the morning, going to the kitchen, eating something, and gazing out the window at the still-dark street with its snowbanks to the knee. I remember how I really did not want to go there, into the darkness, into a cold and strange world. But there was no escape; I had to go. I remember how I was running down the not-yet-lit streets to the metro, very-very fast, because I was very scared. The people around seemed gloomy, evil, and dangerous. I remember how in the metro station, I pressed through the crowd of people who were in a rush to get to work and was always afraid that someone might push me out right onto the tracks. I was looking at that yellow line, beyond which it was forbidden to go under any circumstances and imagined the most horrific scenarios: How I was slipping and sliding beyond this line right under the train; how someone—by accident—pushes me, and I fall head over heels. And sometimes it was the complete opposite—I wanted to go in front of the yellow line and see what would happen, just because I was too tired to be afraid. I remember while sitting in one of the train's cars, that I wanted to talk to someone, share my thoughts, tell how much I did not want to go to school, and how much I wanted to sleep.

There were days, too, that I would constantly turn my head back, hoping to see my mother there. It seemed to me that she was hiding behind someone else's back, and if I looked carefully, I would see her. It seemed as though she was only kidding, pulling a joke on me, and that in reality she was back there, watching me, making sure all was right. And I pretended that I would see her, yell, "Mommy!", run to her, and we would continue the journey together. And I would feel so good, because it was not I who asked her to follow me—I was going to school as if nothing happened—but she herself wanted to watch over me. I had nothing to do with it. I was still the same independent and mature girl. I was just happy to see my mother, I wanted to be with her, and she with me. Yes, I really wanted to feel that, in the right moment, my mother would take me by the hand and go together with me, even if only for a little bit. I wanted to turn around and she would be there, waiting for my signal—waiting for when I would get tired of being independent and mature, and she would come to me right away. Just like that, and not because I cannot manage on my own. I would manage. I just did not want to deal with it by myself. Yes, she would come, without criticizing me and without scolding me for distracting her from her own important independent journey. She would come gladly, as if that is the way it is supposed to be in life.

Of course, I never told my mother any of these thoughts. Probably because I did not want to upset, disappoint, or distract her. I know for sure that my mother would not remain indifferent if I told her. But it seemed to me that I could not tell her this. I just wanted her to feel it and understand everything correctly herself. But she was only human and I was only a child who wanted to have my needs filled without having to ask for them.

Unfortunately, after my first experience with independent life, I kept looking for my mother in the crowd for a long time. Darting from side-to-side, I looked but could not find her. I agonized from loneliness. I suffered, torn apart by the desire to be independent and mature and at the same time to cling to my mother and never leave her side. Later I projected these feeling onto other people in my life. I always tried to be independent, and yet always felt myself dependent. I relied on that look I would feel on my back, on the desire to turn around and see that I was not alone, that there was someone dear to me, waiting for me to call him or her. And, like my mother, that person would have to guess that I was tired of being independent and mature and that I needed help. Of course, I could not say this aloud; I could not ask for this.

This dependency oppressed me so much—until I realized one thing: Only I can free myself from this tangle, this web of dependency and independence. Neither my mother, nor anyone else could help me here, unfortunately. So, I started from the very beginning to solve this problem. I began with a question to that girl inside me, who was not used to showing her true feelings and thoughts and who pretended that she could handle everything by herself. I simply started asking myself before taking a new step, "Are you ready for this? Or do you simply want to seem independent and mature? Catch adoring looks and pretend that you are ready for anything?"

To this day, these simple questions help very much. It gives an opportunity to that independent girl inside me to say, "No." To say that she still needs time to grow up a little. Just a little bit of time, and then she definitely will be ready. I also give her an opportunity to say what she needs to take that new independent step; which inner forces she wants to take with her; who, from her Inner Home, will need to accompany her; who, or what, should be right behind her to come to help her when she might need it. I now realize that I can ask for help because I don't have to deal with everything alone. My independence had become a trap in which I was very dependent. I no longer wish to be in its net. I want to be free to choose whether to walk this part of the journey alone or to ask someone to hold my hand or at least to walk right behind me. It is no longer a dependency, but it is not an independence either. I call this co-dependency.

How I use this word does not have the negative associations attributed to it by the many valuable 12-Step programs. This word, co-dependency, has the connotation of being a free, equal association between two independent people, who can lean on each other when they choose. I treasure that passionately-independent little girl inside me, and she treasures my care and guardianship. We listen to and feel each other—not because we need to, but because we want to be together. We willingly choose to be connected to each other and be co-dependent.

My Inner Housekeeper always has words of wisdom based on what he observes.

I watch over your journey and see how you build in your Inner Home an imaginary corridor with mirrors. You walk along it, trying to decide which door to open and into which room to peak, while still exploring your inner space. You are going by yourself, you are responsible for your choice and journey. Sometimes you look into a mirror, trying to see from the corner of your eye if there is someone behind you. Before, there were only shadows—a shadow of your mother, the shadows of the people on whose help you counted, your grudges and disappointments in people. Now, behind your back there is your experience, your discovered strengths and resources, wisdom of the past generations, and the real, close-to-you people. And if you need help on the outside, you can simply ask for it, because now you allow yourself to not be fully prepared for the next step.

You now give yourself a chance to grow up and show your real independence only when you are ready for it. You no longer need to prove to anyone that you can manage on your own. You know that you can handle it by yourself. And that is why you ask for help, offer it, give someone a hand, or lean on someone. You allow yourself to be co-dependent and connected to other people not because you need to, but because you consciously choose to. Continue to go along this endless corridor in your Inner Home, opening more new doors and spaces. Listen to the little girl inside you, who so wants to do everything herself. Yet, be sure that she can always stop, look back, and ask for help from someone who is only a couple of steps behind and who accompanies her attentively and caringly.

On the Way to
Choosing Growth over Perfection

I first began seriously to consider my pursuit of perfection when I saw my youngest daughter choosing plush toys. She would look at the shelf full of toys and always get excited about one that had a little, almost unnoticeable, flaw or, in the language of adults, a defect. She would tell me, "Look how cute this doggy is! It has one eye a little crooked, and all the others have their eyes straight and all the same. I want this one, the special one. Look at how this bunny's one ear is to the side, and all the others' ears are straight up. I want this bunny, the real one, and all the others are fake, there are no bunnies like that in real life." I was completely stunned by such an exact and true observation my daughter had made. So, for the first time in my life, I asked myself, "What do I really want to be—perfect and fake or imperfect and real?" To me, the answer was obvious, "I want to be real!" But how to accept my own imperfections; how to get rid of the ever-present and often subconscious desire to be ideal and perfect in everything? How to accept myself as an imperfect and incomplete creation?

Since by that time I was already sufficiently experienced in untying my own tight inner knots, I patiently started at the very beginning. I asked myself, "What is this desire to be ideal and perfect? Why do I need it so much? Most importantly, how true is this desire to me, to my own nature? Or, maybe it was acquired because of the life circumstances I had encountered that made this desire a life necessity, a second nature?"

The answers I found in myself were very surprising: I found out that although the need to be perfect is not helpful in any way, the desire for perfection was not born inside me just because; it had a very important root that I didn't want just to get rid of. I realized that deep down two very strong and natural impulses struggled within me—to be more precise, several desirable forms of being.

First, I was looking for a perfect, complete and constant form, without flaws. That is, a divine form. This is the form that I have never seen but have wished for since my childhood years. I had been picturing this form in my imagination, subconsciously reaching for it, and yet completely depriving it of its humanity (that is, of the human limitations). Hence, this form only remained in my imagination, although the pressure of this image was very real.

At the same time, I longed for a feeling of being enough the way I am at this exact moment; to feel my growth and changes and accept myself in this unformed and sometimes even unnamed form. In other words, to be a divine being—that is, a complete, formed, perfect creation—and yet to feel my humanity and incompleteness. I wanted to be god and human at the same time. I was able to see so clearly the way I had always longed for the divine in me and at the same time, for the feeling of humanity. By themselves, these desires and searches are wonderful. However, just as it usually happens, I got confused in my quest, lost my direction, and as a result, completely forgot where I started to search and what I was really looking for.

Then I began to think once again about this divine complete form and realized that true divine force is not finite; to the contrary, it is constantly moving and growing. That is, if I really want to get closer to my true divine form, I simply need to allow myself this endless movement forward and above, toward my own divine potential. Now, every movement contains certain limitations—in speed, in external climate conditions, in emptiness or, conversely, with congestion on the road where this movement takes place. If I notice my own imperfections and limitations, accepting them calmly and lovingly like little flags and signs that mark my journey ahead and above, I consistently grow and develop, and hence, I keep my connection with that divine form within me. I become perfect in my human imperfection.

Only when I was able to separate the process of my movement and growth (that divine and natural creative process) from my feeling of being-enough and place them into different spaces of my Inner Home, could I truly get to know and accept them both within me. By accepting my human imperfections, by allowing myself the divine movement ahead and above, and by maintaining the feeling of myself always being "enough", I can feel myself imperfectly real, whole and full of a divine spark. A gift and a relief.

Message from Inner Heart Companion that connects the divinity and humanity within me:

The acceptance of my divinity and humanity is filled with unconditional love and does not ask of me anything in return. This voice simply reminds me softly and tenderly that I am still the same as the day I was born; I am still the same infinite cosmic universe, surrounded by a physical body. I was infinite and complete from the very beginning.

Now I simply know much more about myself and the world around me than back then, in the beginning of the journey. Now I possess human life experience; but my essence, my inner core has not changed and will not change for the rest of my days.

I am always in a state of becoming who I am. The feeling of my own full value has always been, is, and will continue to be present in my Inner Home. My choice is only whether to listen to that feeling with attention and respect, or not.

On the Way to Being Seen and Heard

Oh, how you want the others to look at you, see you! How you yearn to be seen!

When all your thoughts have been heard, all your fantasies and dreams have been expressed out loud, when you can speak and sing using your own voice, even if it is loud, without fearing that someone would scold you, saying that you look ridiculous, have no talent, or that you speak too much and too loudly. When your entire body can express itself freely and naturally and your heart is open, beating steadily and surely. When nobody will close a door in the face of the real and natural you. When you come out on your own stage at any moment, and no one will laugh at you, or throw tomatoes at you, or send you to study more. When you can, at any given moment, open up and share—you can be in the spotlight, natural, free, open, and enjoying this feeling. When you are noticed, not only in that moment when you have found an ideal, perfect form, but in the moment of search. When you are accepted while in this search, and you do not need to hide in embarrassment. When you can walk freely, without hiding in a corner, rehearsing tens of times, and then perform a perfectly revised play. When you are free from expectations. When you simply stand in your spotlight and create, expressing every color of your inner world.

Is it possible then that there is such a space as this on earth that would withstand all your search, expressions, quests and doubts—this growth and development?

I remember how this need to be seen and heard was born in me. When I was ten-eleven years old, I wanted to be a singer. Not become, but be. And it does not matter why I had chosen this creative expression. Maybe because my mom always sang at home with a guitar; maybe because in our home music was always welcome. It does not matter. What matters is that for me this was my first impulse to go out onto my big stage, begin my journey as a creator. I remember playing the songs of different singers, singing and dancing to them. And, of course, I wanted to show them to my mom, because I needed someone to see and hear me in my search, someone to witness the whole process. I was not able at the time to observe myself from outside—this is hard at any time but at eleven years old, it was impossible. I needed another pair of eyes and ears—not just any, but the ones closest to me. I did not need a director, a screenwriter, or a critic. I needed a mute witness who would not judge me, would not expect anything of me, but rather would simply watch me attentively, with love and care, and maybe sometimes applaud me for support. Unfortunately, my mom did not handle this role well, simply because she was not aware of my need, simply because I could not tell her about my true needs. And yet, she tried hard. She sat and watched me, gave me her comments and director decisions (she is also a TV director by training, so it was natural for her). And I saw that she was trying and felt that it would be somehow impolite to get mad at her, no matter how angry I was beginning to feel. Remaining with me to this day is the verdict she gave me after one of my apparently not-so-good performances: "Well, it is obvious that you will never be Alla Pugachova (a famous Russian singer). So, why do this in the first place then? Come on, you are a smart girl." Now I clearly see that my mom was trying to end my, and her own, suffering and put my energy in the right direction. But what I understood from those words and remembered for the rest of my life was that I completely lacked talent. And it did not matter that she was only talking about my singing—I felt that I had been singing very well, but if mom said that it was mediocre, then I had created an illusion for myself, a fantasy. In other words, my inner system of defining my talents and abilities is defective. It does not work.

After that, for many years whenever it seemed to me that I was doing something with great talent or very expressively, immediately there was a doubt crawling in and the burning questions, "Are these not fantasies? Can it be that you imagined a fairy-tale for yourself, but in reality, you are worthless?" Later even when others would say something nice about my expression, I did not take it seriously. With time it only became worse. I no longer wanted to get onto my imaginary stage. Or, deep inside I, of course, wanted to, but it felt so uncomfortable and frightening. And most importantly, the picture I was presenting seemed so blurry, like in a haze—was I good or not, with talent or not? As a result, I had stopped performing at home completely, and abandoned any attempt at creating for many years. I looked for opportunities to be creative in various external expressions, but inside I did not feel creative anymore.

The next lesson I took away from this experience was perfectionism. I would tell myself, "If you start doing something, do it in the perfect way possible (at least like Pugachova). Otherwise, it is not worth to even try." But here is a subsequent question that, unfortunately, dawned on me only many years later, "How can one arrive to this perfect result if one does not try, search, attempt, reach out to the higher level gradually, going through all the stages?" Of course, there are geniuses born who pick up a violin at a young age and start playing right off. But even they never stop practicing if they hope to achieve a high level. So, in my fearful and convoluted thinking, it seemed that it only made sense to do something that for sure would go well. And since I did not know what would go well, I did not try anything. On the outside it appeared to others that I tried. But in reality, I did not try, search, explore, practice, or create. I sat in a corner and watched others on the stage, convincing myself that they had much more talent, were brighter and more original. And, of course, whatever they did was brilliant right away. I did not even allow myself to envy them because I had so-called high moral principles. I simply suffered and thought how lucky they were. My reasoning and thoughts to myself went something like this, "They are blessed, the chosen ones. They have the right to go onto their own stage in life. And I am merely a spectator."

The final lesson, or caution, I took away from my first conscious creative experience was that it was dangerous to be seen, noticed, and bright because I did not know how the audience would react, how it would judge. I saw the whole scenario in my mind's eye: Standing at that moment on the stage, vulnerable and sensitive, creating something and trying to express the most intimate and sacred part of myself, the one that is deep inside, patiently waiting for it to emerge. There are lights everywhere; everyone is watching and waiting. But then, one person moves or maybe makes an unpleasant face or looks away. He does not have to say anything, but it crushes the most tender and inviolate part that I had tried to show. Yes, this is the scene that has played out over the years and I came away with the admonition, "It is best not to stick your head out. It is safer this way."

Later, as I was growing up, I gave myself many logical explanations as to why I could not be seen and heard. Some of these reasons (or excuses) were, "I am by nature shy. I do not like to attract attention. I let the others have all the spotlight because I am kind and I do not envy. Not everyone should be in the spotlight, some need to be in the shadow." And if suddenly I found myself accidentally in the spotlight, I felt so terribly guilty. I then would tell myself: "I am taking someone else's place, taking away someone else's attention. After all, I do not need that stage, I already know my worth. Do I really need to prove anything to anyone?"

But it turned out that I did. Not to the people around me and not even to my mom, who did not wish me anything bad. But to myself. I needed to convince myself that I could be seen, that I deserved to be in the center of the circle, in the spotlight. And it had nothing to do with some creative ambition; rather, it had to do with the fact that it is a natural human developmental need—to be seen and to be heard by your own self.

In our Inner Home, simply a stage is necessary, some sort of a creative studio where we can search, try, create, make mistakes and search again, expressing ourselves naturally and independently of the results. All this is done just in the name of the creative process. All I needed from my mom in my childhood was that she would be a silent spectator, a witness to my creative search. Seemingly, it was so little, and yet, it was so much. All I needed from myself was to hear and accept my own need to be seen and heard. This, too, seemed so little—and, yet again, it was so much. I myself needed to witness my creative search and build my own inner stage where I could be vulnerable, sensual, passionate, open in all of my expressions—anything I wanted to be. I myself needed to stand on that stage freely and naturally, feeling that I am in the right place, meaning a place that rightfully belongs to me.

A message from my Inner Housekeeper:

Your journey to your inner stage is winding and, by far, not easy. On this journey, you have to go through many fears, much resistance, shame, resentment and anger, doubt and suffering. On this journey, it is very easy to give up, hide, convince yourself of the failure and senselessness of that very movement, that impulse to be seen and heard. And, only by allowing yourself to experiment with and experience that natural need and vital necessity, will you truly be able to see and hear yourself. By permitting yourself this inner movement, expression, desire, idea, creative spark—without looking back at the audience, judging yourself, or chasing a specific result— you allow yourself to become the creator of your inner (and, hence, your outer) world. You become a part of a creative flow of life that carries you on its wave, washing away all the unnecessary guilt and trauma that stuck to you over the years—whatever it is that prevents you from swimming freely, naturally, and safely.

Permitting this, you find yourself in your own inner spotlight that illuminates before you everything that is ready to be expressed. You become your main spectator, silent and attentive to the unfolding creative journey. Your inner stage awaits you and you just need to allow yourself the desire to get onto it.

Setting Up My Own Inner Clock

No matter what your destination is right now,
you are always on The Way Home.

On the Way
to
My Own Timing

When I was a little girl, my mom kept telling me that the most important thing in life is patience. I do not remember much of my early childhood, but this I recall very clearly. For example, we are sitting in a line to see a doctor, and I start whining about being tired. And then my mother asks me in a very conspiracy-like manner, "Do you remember what the most important thing in life is?" And I respond, "Patience!" And for some reason, I calm down right away. Later, I asked my mom many times, from where she got that phrase (especially given that she herself was never particularly known for being patient), but to this day she cannot give me an answer to this question. It was as if this phrase came to her from somewhere above, or was dictated to her by some sort of maternal instinct.

One way or another, this phrase became the greatest gift I ever got from my mother because it is precisely this patience that helps me, and at times saves me, in my life journey. I think that everything that I am today, everything that comprises my inner universe, my Inner Home, came to me because of patience. Patience is my true strength and treasure. And yet, I always felt that I never had enough of it in life. How I often wished that I would not have to wait and go through the entire journey all over again; I wish I were able to rush the time, take a detour, accelerate, pass, run ahead. It seems that I do not have the specific patience necessary for such waiting and I want to explode and scream, "Come on! How long do I have to wait?" And only after having gone through a particular part of a journey from the beginning to the end and patiently overcoming a given situation, would I realize how important it was not to hurry and not to rush the process. I also saw that with each such experience, my patience grew bigger and stronger. I mean, every time I had a little more patience than what the situation required, and after having gone through that situation, I thus expanded the boundaries of my patience. Thanks to this extra patience, it made my further journey much easier. Most importantly, with each new experience, my faith in patience grew stronger. Whenever I go through a rough patch in life, I feel confused, scared, and sometimes unable to bear the situation, I repeat to myself my mother's word— "patience." I assure myself, "Just be patient and everything will somehow get resolved. Even the most difficult time eventually comes to an end. And the more patience you use in this time, the more you receive and discover in the end."

All the while, a very interesting phenomenon developed. With time, thanks to the patience cultivated in me, my Inner Home came to have its own subjective perception of time. It was as if I received as a gift, an internal clock that was synchronized to my inner truth, my nature, my pace, my journey. This clock harmonized my personal need of timing for a specific process, regardless of the accepted norms or other people's time estimations. It was as though my patience received, as a support, an inner synchrony or inner timing that did not rush, but rather helped me to accept the time allowed for a particular process, independent of how quickly or slowly the same process took for the people around me. The most interesting thing was that, when I stopped rushing myself and showed some patience with myself and my processes, I started to move through life much more quickly than before. My journey became more active and intense, but only because of my inner preparedness and not due to some external pressure and impatience.

For example, In the process of writing this book, periodically I would catch myself thinking, "How I wish to finish this, spill everything out, share, read it aloud to someone, be there at the finish line." And, of course, it was not possible. As soon as I would start to rush myself, my journey would lose its entire meaning, and the very process would lose its value. So again, I would resign myself and patiently accept my inner timing, my inner watch and patience that was trying to make my journey easier. I had to believe, once more, in the strength of the very process, the very journey, and stoically wait until my patience would grow with me and bring me to a cogent conclusion of this journey and a beginning of a new one. And if I really wanted to whine as I did when I was little, I would ask myself: "What is most important in life?" And I would answer: "Patience." And, for some reason, I would feel much more at ease right away.

Regarding patience, this message comes from my Inner Personal Assistant:

Your patience became your true strength and an infinite resource that grows within you and helps you to express your truth, to complete different processes, to develop your ideas, and to commit to what is truly important to you. This sense of your own inner timing allows you to stay true and natural and recognize and respect another's pace. When you take a breath and trust your inner wise and accurate clock, you find yourself exactly in the right place at the right time.

On the Way to Being Loyal and Committed to Myself

I have been exploring these questions for a very long time: Why is it so hard to commit to ourselves, to stay loyal to our True Self? Why is it so easy to *not* keep a promise we give ourselves? Why is it more important and easier to be committed to others than our own true needs? I have come to some realizations that I would like to share with you through this imaginary short story:

There is a family celebration and everyone is in a festive mood, ready to party. But it so happens that the youngest girl in the family wakes up in a very sad and worried mood. It does not matter why, it just happens so. She, of course, wants to be hugged, cuddled, and calmed. But everyone around is busy with the celebration, which is completely understandable. Then the girl, having acted up a bit, realizes that today she will not get the attention she needs from the adults. And so she decides to help herself. She crawls under the blanket and indulges her sorrow; she listens to some sad music, draws something sad, or simply plays with her favorite toy. There are many possibilities. Yet, everyone around suddenly gets worried, if not frustrated. The expressions may vary, "Why are you so sad when we are celebrating?" "Why are you lying in bed, do you not value our effort?" "We all are ready to celebrate or already celebrating, and only you are ruining everyone's mood with your long face." And a most popular one, "Can you at least once in your life think of someone other than yourself?" And so forth. And so, the girl gets up from the bed, puts on a dress, pulls a smile onto her face, and comes out to celebrate together with the others. Possibly, she eventually will even have fun, and then her mother, pleased, will tell her, "You see? I told you. I know what's best for you. You would have stayed in your room and suffered all by yourself. Now, isn't this better?"

But what the mother does not know is that the suffering began for this little girl the moment she put on that fake smile because in that moment she betrayed herself. She chose a commitment to others, and thus broke a precious promise, given to her by nature, to be true to herself. Just a couple of minutes previous it seemed so easy. She was herself, did not ask anyone for anything, did not bother anyone, did not fight for anything. She was simply true to herself and her inner needs that, most likely, would change very soon anyway, and the girl would want to have fun instead of being sad. But as soon as she chose herself, the adults around her began to have their own inner needs that had been left unanswered, perhaps for years—pain, disappointment, sometimes even anger and resentment from endless betrayals of themselves. So, they hurriedly turned off those feelings and simply told the child, "Stop being sad and come celebrate with us." And the girl heard, "Stop being true and loyal to yourself because you don't belong here when you choose yourself."

The child listened to them—problem solved and the celebration can go on. But, the adults, perhaps sensing their own inner, thwarted child, promise themselves good things: "Starting Monday, I will eat healthily; will spend more quality time with my child; will definitely read the book/watch the movie I have been meaning to read/watch for so long. Maybe I will even fulfill my old dream, or at least start planning how to fulfill it." Tomorrow does come and all these promises seem like an impossible task, not very important, or even devoid of any sense. And it is not because we are weak, lazy, do not have will power, or do not love ourselves. It is because betraying ourselves, denying our own needs, doubting the importance of our own desires has become second nature—a habit that requires unimaginable strength to overcome.

When I came to this realization and started listening to my inner stories of self-betrayal, I felt a strong need to commit to every wish and demand that arose inside me. I felt that I owed it to myself. But soon enough, another important question came upon me: How can I understand which of those desires are my own and true, and which ones were imposed on me by those around me, the society, external standards? If it comes to expending my efforts on achieving goals, making wishes come true, satisfying inner needs, it is important to make sure that they are mine. I was done with being loyal to everyone's else needs.

It turned out that the first thing that needed to be achieved on my way to being loyal and devoted to myself was honesty and the desire to hear the truth, even if it was uncomfortable and did not fit into the picture of life I created. If we were to continue the example with the little girl, we can imagine that she grows up, she is doing well, no serious drama in her life. She organizes parties and celebrations. You may ask why. And she will happily tell you that in her family, the celebrations were always the best. She will say, "My parents knew how to celebrate any event so that no one would feel left out. Everyone participated and had fun, kids and adults alike. So, I, too, decided to bring happiness to others, especially since I know about celebrations more than anyone and am so good at it."

But, what we do not see, is that after every such party, this grown up girl returns home, crawls under the blanket, and feels sorry for herself. Sometimes she cries; sometimes eating something that later causes a stomachache; sometimes she gets so angry at the whole world that sparks fly. And then one day she decides to be honest with herself and asks the questions that have been really bothering her, "So, what is wrong with me? Everything is great, I have a job that I love and do so well. Why am I feeling so bad, as if I did something wrong, betrayed someone or lied? Why am I so angry and sad, why am I feeling guilty?"

We know the truth and answers to these questions, since we see her story objectively from the beginning. But for her to remember her feelings and the actions of her parents she would need much time and, most likely, numerous therapy sessions. But even if she will find that truth, obviously she cannot change the past, and it is not her parents' fault—they did what they thought was best. So, what good does this truth?

Here is the explanation that I have come to see as legitimate. This grown girl does not have to do an exploration or investigation of her entire life and dig for truth or reasons. Correcting the past happens in the present. Therefore, she can be honest with herself right this minute and say, "Right now, I am not okay, I am sad. And it does not matter why; it does not matter that everyone around is celebrating. What matters is that I know that right now I am sad. I will no longer betray my sadness; rather, I will remain on its side. I will simply accept it as a given." It may seem like such a little thing, as if nothing really happened. Nothing got solved, and there are no new answers. But in reality, so much happened. The girl, for the first time in many years, *has* made a different choice. She chose to remain loyal to the need she felt at that moment. She honestly told herself, "I want to be sad." And then she asked herself, "In which way do I want to be sad?" Today maybe she will stay lying down under the blanket; tomorrow she might want to listen to sad songs and cry, etc. Essentially, through current behavior and awareness, she has corrected the past. And with each day that passes, this sadness will become lighter and she will be happier because that little girl, within the grown woman, will finally get what she needed. She was able to express freely and naturally her emotions without betraying herself and having remorse in front of others; just to be herself, to be truthful to herself and her inner nature. Eventually, she will want celebrate and enjoy this celebration sincerely and truly, not because she must or should.

It may be very difficult to make such a choice in favor of ourselves, because it may bring misunderstanding from those around us. This choice might appear to be disrespectful of laws, norms, or accepted rules. With these external pressures and unspoken criticisms, our promises to ourselves drift, even strengthening the feelings of guilt, shame and anger. We destroy the entire foundation of our Inner Home because we do not believe that loyalty to ourselves is real or makes sense.

Taking a similar tack on a more societal level, it seems today that many do not believe in faithfulness of spouses, a devotion to whatever one does, to family, or country. The question arises, "How is it possible to believe if each of us betrays on the daily basis himself and his own nature?" The conclusion then may be that faithfulness becomes a weighty task for an individual human nature.

But if we would only imagine that inside each of us there is a home—the Inner Home that I talk about throughout this book—where there are many different and unique rooms. And even if we are unfamiliar with every corner of that home and do not know what is in the closets and on the faraway shelves, this home is all we really have. It is our treasure and it is worth fighting for. It is what we want to be devoted and faithful to because only this world is truly ours. If we look at this home as we would our material home that houses our bodies, we can see the necessity of taking care of its problems and general maintenance. This care requires constant monitoring, with clear eyes and an open heart.

For me, being faithful and devoted to my Inner Home, to one's self, one's own promises, values, and desires is true connection, true belonging. It is the intimacy with one's self and the people around us. Subsequently, he who is loyal to his Inner Home will respect the loyalty of another. He who acknowledges the value of his own needs and desires will not lay his eyes on another's. He who is honest and loyal to his truth will accept that of the other. He who has taken at least one step toward himself, stepped onto the road toward his Inner Home, known true connection, will be able to express this truth to another.

By reclaiming that priceless agreement of loyalty and devotion to myself that was given to me at birth, I can be honest and true to my needs, dreams, goals, tasks, life lessons, and people around me.

The message from my Inner Housekeeper keeps me focused on my truth:

You always know your truth—sometimes it is deep inside, and sometimes it is on the surface. You always know when you betray yourself. You cannot hide that truth. It shows through different symptoms in your body, your thoughts, your dreams, your heart, your soul. You know! By paying attention to these symptoms, you can stop that betrayal in any moment and make a different choice—one in favor of your inner truth. Every such choice will become a step on this big journey, and at some point, you will no longer be able to betray yourself. Betrayal will stop being your habit, your second nature, because you will have only one true nature. Being true and devoted to yourself will no longer require an effort; it will become a natural life expression.

You cannot leave this journey. You cannot run away from yourself. Your choice is only about how you will make this journey—curl up in a ball, hide your face and feel yourself a liar and traitor, or with your back straight, open gaze, your head raised with dignity, knowing that you stayed true and loyal to your Inner Home.

On the Way

to

My True Self

Over the course of my life, I discovered that, to many people, truth is like an ice-cold shower—invigorating and reviving, but not always comfortable, and even shocking at times. We hear about how healthy it is to take cold showers, how stimulating, strengthening, and healing they are. However, not everyone chooses to take such a shower each day. The hardest part is actually to start, to make a first step into the cold stream of water, knowing that the discomfort will pass and we will feel the refreshment and the strength of our body. In this same way, when we choose to make an inner movement and hear even a small amount of inner truth, we start feeling the purity and strength of our inner core, our soul.

Like many other children, I was always told how important it is to tell the truth. To me, this seemingly simple rule always brought with it a mixture of various meanings and values—the so-called double standards. Even as a child, I came to several disappointing conclusions, based my own experience. First, by telling my truth to those around me, I risked hearing that my truth was incorrect, silly, senseless, or even completely false. Second, when telling the truth, I ought to always consider the feelings of those to whom I was telling it, as my truth could offend someone and cause me a great deal of trouble. Finally, and most important, it is extremely difficult to tell, or to hear, the truth regarding oneself; it is uncomfortable, and sometimes very painful.

By asking adults uncomfortable questions and expecting truthful answers from them, I saw that they would get lost and confused and try to finish this uncomfortable conversation as soon as possible. It was as if I had put them under an icy shower, and they tried to get out of it as quickly as they could, angry and annoyed at my persistence. With time, I, too, began to shy away from and even fear truth because it seemed to me that my honest direct response or a sincere expression could shock those around me and give me that unpleasant feeling of shame, as if something is wrong with me or I am not doing it right. It was as if I was breaking some long-established and well-known rules.

Gradually, I also learned to play by the rules. I learned to masterfully tell people what they wanted to hear; distort the truth so that everyone around would be comfortable. I learned to fit into any situation and any company. Finally, I learned to hide my inner truth from myself. I learned to lie, fake, dodge, and confuse myself, so that the uncomfortable truth would not surface under any circumstances.

While the external truth can reach us anywhere and anytime, the inner truth, I believe, only comes out when we are safe enough to hear it or can no longer hide it from ourselves. In either case, we are usually ready for it. On the way to my true self, I discovered new laws and rules that turned out to be very simple and clear, just like the very nature of truth. In the process of discovering my inner truth, I am not required to separate it into good and bad; I do not need to go to extremes by either trying to tell myself everything at once, or by keeping quiet and pretending that there is no truth at all. I do not need to wonder about how I will perceive this truth simply because my inner defense mechanisms will not allow me to learn what I am not supposed to know just yet. The inner truth can be different or difficult, but it always brings relief, calmness, and healing. It can excite, cause discomfort or even pain. It can warm, cleanse, and fill with new strength. But most importantly, this shower of truth is located in my Inner Home—and hence, it is always in sync with my inner nature and being. I do not need to know how to turn this shower on or how to regulate it; I only need the desire to open this well of truth inside me. The amount of pressure and the temperature will always be those for which I am ready that day.

I think that I began my conscious journey toward my truth, my true self when my first child was born. Looking at my son—so pure, innocent, and true—I suddenly realized that I, too, wanted to be the same way and that I would simply not be able to be a good mother for him if I would not be true, natural and real. Such sincere and true desire was enough to open this pure well of truth inside me and let it, drop by drop, gradually cleanse me and bring me back Home, to my true self. Years have passed since that moment, and I have discovered an enormous amount of truth, both about myself and the world around me. There were days when I did not want to hear this truth or feel it (somewhat similar to when little children sometimes do not want to get into the shower), but after standing for some time under this spring of truth pouring over me, I have always felt relief, liberation, and purification. Eventually I became accustomed to this procedure. Truth became a natural and vital life component for me. I try to spend as much time as possible under its streams and greatly appreciate how clearly I can now see myself and my journey.

Today, I feel that I can regulate my inner shower of truth and release the amount that each person can handle, without dousing them with an ice-cold stream, but rather only giving them a chance to refresh. I am no longer afraid of hurting someone with my truth because I feel that inside me it is always warm and pure, and therefore, cannot do anyone any harm. I no longer have double standards in terms of truth because now I am certain that the truth that comes from my Inner Home will always be better and more important that any most beautifully created story or conveniently distorted reality.

Today, I can tell my children sincerely and truthfully that it is very important to tell the truth, listen to their own truth and respect it. But most important, I can teach it to them through my own example: by showing that even the shower that was once only bringing ice-cold water and seemed repelling and unapproachable, with time can become warm and calming. This will be so if the shower comes from their Inner Home and is filled with their own truth.

A message from my Inner Heart Companion concerning my Truth:

When I am true, my mind is peaceful and quiet, my body is relaxed and grounded, my heart is full of love and gratitude. I feel as if everything is right with the world. I feel that everything is right with me, that it is safe being me, that I love being myself. When I am true, I feel pure and clear. I feel connected, fulfilled, strong and natural. When I am true, I feel at Home with myself.

My Private Rooms:
Inner Gym, Altar, Playroom, Library

No matter what your destination is right now,
you are always on The Way Home.

On the Way to Taking Good Care of My Anger

Anger is one of the dark colors that sometimes appears in my Inner Home. It happens not because someone makes me angry; it happens regardless of how happy and inspired I am. I get angry because I am human. I choose to be a real live person who accepts my entire spectrum of colors, given to me by nature. Every one of those colors is precious and invaluable to me, and I do not divide them into bad and good ones. I know all my clearest, pure, and inspired tones, as well as the darkest, blazing and rich shades. I know my light and my darkness. They are intertwined and neither would exist without the other. In my Inner Home there is space for all my feelings, even the ones so uncomfortable and unpleasant as anger. More than that, very often, I find my anger very useful because facing and exploring it gives me an opportunity to see what is behind it. Usually, I find there an important piece of information or a hidden feeling that is precious to me. I love all my colors because they are what makes me, me.

In my childhood home, it was not customary to say aloud things like, "I am angry" or "I am angry with you." This feeling was thoroughly hidden, but nonetheless it still would come out in unexpected and powerful outbursts of anger. Since the process of someone getting angry was not clearly understood, such outbursts took me completely by surprise. For example, I could not understand how and when my parents would begin getting angry, I could not follow the process of boiling, it was carefully hidden, because getting angry was wrong. But yelling at each other— that is, spilling out all that anger with absolutely no control was considered normal. Just like that, I myself did not want to and could not notice how my anger was growing inside and spilling out, discouraging me and leaving a heavy feeling of guilt, but at the same time also leaving a feeling of relief because it was finally free. That is, by avoiding and ignoring my anger and suppressing it I was only getting under its influence more. My refusal of the anger only fueled it more, and to understand the nature of this simple, yet powerful feeling, was becoming more difficult.

In reality, everything would have been much easier if we were allowed to get angry. If we could let our anger out for a couple of minutes every day, like brushing our teeth or going to the bathroom—that is, as a measure of personal hygiene. It would have been wonderful to learn that anger is natural without being afraid that the feeling would destroy us or make us bad. We would have learned to simply let those emotions out, without suppressing them and without condemning ourselves. We learned the natural process of bowel movements to cleanse our bodies, even though nothing pretty or beautiful happens there, rather the opposite. We accept this process as natural and simply let it happen. So, why do we view anger as such a destructive force? Why do we not allow this feeling to be expressed in its natural form (often much smaller than what we imagine), fighting it instead, thus increasing its might and turning it from a simple dark color into a true fire-breathing poisonous dragon?

In our childhood, when the feelings are not yet suppressed and accumulated like a snowball, but are let out freely and naturally, it is much easier to do. So often I can see a child crying and throwing an angry tantrum, and a minute later this child calms down and does not even remember why he was angry. Children do not spend time trying to control their emotions and simply let them out; that is why their emotions pass much faster. Because any motion has its beginning and end, and the freer the motion, the faster it ends, giving way to a new one.

But what to do when this unexpressed anger was suppressed for years, turning into fury and aggression? An anger that stopped being just waste easy to throw away or a temporary flash, but turned instead into time bombs? As a result of this long inner suppression, many of us are forced to tiptoe through a minefield, afraid to accidentally touch a bomb and explode ourselves, or others. We may find ourselves living in fear, worry, or even have panic attacks, thinking that, suddenly, something will get out of our control, and no one will then be safe. We have often heard that anger is bad for our health, makes us unhappy, prevents us from getting closer to other people and building healthy relationships. Consequently, if we continue to get angry and let that anger out, we may remain forever alone and miserable.

So, it seems that we do not have a choice, that if we want to be happy, in a healthy relationship and live "right", we need to stop getting angry. In theory, it sounds very logical, however, I offer this caveat—only if you are not human, but a bodiless spiritual creature that is only filled with light and unconditional love. A divine creation, devoid of everything human. This line of thinking pushes me to ask those who believe in suppressing anger, "Do you really think that if I, with the force of my will, can convince myself that getting angry is bad, my anger will simply evaporate, disappear? If I get angry, does it automatically deny me an opportunity to remain full of divine purity?"

For me, the answer is very clear. I want to remain a real person who walks with her feet on the ground; a person who is true and devoted to her human nature, as well as her spiritual, energetic, and cosmic nature; a person who is true to her human purpose of uniting in her the most divine and earthy, the dark and the light, no matter how difficult it may be at times. This is why my anger deserves that I at least acknowledge its right to be. It exists, whether I want it or not.

So, instead of enslaving it, waging a war against it, or avoiding it, I can invite it into my Inner Home and simply listen to its story. If it is an emotion without a lengthy tale, it receives my attention almost immediately upon appearing. Then it will calmly walk out of my home, the same way it had walked in. This routine will be my personal intimate activity, like going to the restroom, that no one will know about, or it will be accepted as a part of a natural process.

If, on the other hand, my anger has been waiting for this conversation for years, then this dialogue can take on a very aggressive tone. Hence, to make sure that this conversation is safe for both of us, I should consider the right, safe space with clear boundaries. If my anger is literally spewing over as soon as I get close, then it must have numerous reasons to do so. The first thing I can do for my anger is to allow it to let the steam out, because until that happens, there will be no productive conversation. Following this story line, it might be good if every home could have a special punching bag that will handle this kind of aggression, thus giving anger a chance not to spill over onto others and myself, avoiding to become a punching bag myself. In my Inner Home there is a safe, well-equipped gym, where I can run, jump, yell, fight, and express the anger accumulated in me.

It is interesting that as soon as I, with the help of my imagination, created this safe inner space where my anger could feel at home and be itself, I basically stopped feeling the need to pour these feelings out. Once my anger found a free and safe container where it could be as intense as it wanted, it calmed down very quickly and was no longer a destructive force. Listening to its story, I soon realized that behind this anger were sadness, pain, guilt, and fear of rejection.

I can say now that my dark colors no longer scare me, nor anger, being its leader, because it has become a part of my home, a natural part of me. It has been accepted inside me along with other beautiful feelings—it is no better, no worse. I know that when I am attentive and empathic to the story that lies behind my anger, it opens to me from a different angle, helping me be stronger, truer, and deeper. Most importantly, it helps me remain a real person, a divine being with a human experience. A human who is able to contain the dark and the light within.

Message from my Inner Heart Companion:

In my heart, I can feel empathy and true care for my anger. I can feel how much fear, shame and sadness usually hide behind this strong and powerful emotion. I can imagine my anger being very scared even when it seems furious or even aggressive. I can feel how much my anger wants to be included and accepted, how it is afraid to be rejected. I want to give my anger a hand, to listen to its story, to step into its shoes, to see and understand it. I want to be kind toward my anger, to take a good care of it and to bring it Home.

Then I can feel the relief, the calmness and the richness that my anger brings with it, just because it was finally invited and welcomed. I can feel that my anger becomes just a color, not better and not worse, just another color that makes my Inner Home a whole, united, rich and peaceful space.

On the Way to My True Love

I believe that inside each of us there an unlimited amount of love; the kind of love that travels throughout our inner space like a first responder, ready to come to the rescue of the part that needs it the most. It is the love that heals, fills and elevates our nature unconditionally. It is the love that does not scream, but rather calmly, patiently and consistently completes its task. It possesses a magical force and is well aware of it but does not brag about it. It is full of dignity, empathy, and sincerity. As any magical force, love has a secret place, perhaps a small chest in which love's seed is kept, its source of power, its core. From this source, love sends and spreads its waves and streams. That is also where love receives impulses that accumulate its energy and create wider and deeper waves. That small chest is our heart.

My heart is the central part of my body, of my inner nature, and much of my inner structure depends on how free, natural, and safe my heart feels. My heart is not just the engine that ensures life functions of the body, but also the core of my inner universe. It is the starting point, the very birthplace of all the alive, human and natural that exists in me.

Love has always been the most important component of my life; both when I was looking for it in the outside world, and when I found its source in my Inner Home. Love, in its many forms, was always vital

179

to me, like air, without which I would start to suffocate.

The first love I ever felt and absorbed was the love of my parents for me. My mother's love was very strong, felt by my every cell, warming, giving strength, but it was also inconsistent, like a roller coaster. It was also addictive, with me becoming hostage to these emotions and dependent on the adrenaline rush and pleasure I got. Yet, I felt that this love was opening the best and strongest in me, and that is why it is impossible to refuse. It gives and takes away at the same time.

My father's love was completely different. It was quiet, contained, more introverted than showing on the outside. It did not fill me up like my mother's love, but it did not leave me empty either. It was a stable love, not always felt, but giving confidence and support. What united these two different forms of love in me was that they both felt as conditional. That is, of course, I realize that my parents always loved me, regardless of anything, but on the surface, it was expressed—or perceived by me—as a love with an immense number of conditions and rules. And only by following them I felt that I was worthy and deserving of that love.

As time passed, I realized how difficult it is to express your love unconditionally. It is nearly impossible, especially when it comes to expressing this love in the relationship with those closest to us. That is why I know that my parents have given me the most love that they were able to give, a beautiful and very profound love, and I have long since given up any complaints. Yet, to me the most important thing in love has always been crystal-clear truth first and foremost with myself. While in other aspects I could fake, pretend, confuse, or even mislead myself, love was always something sacred for me. Here, I was not open to any concessions, compromises, falseness, or half-truths. Love was my only beacon, my fortress that I was not willing to give up no matter the pressure. I fought for it and protected the love in my heart like a lioness, not allowing anyone to tarnish or belittle its importance for me. It was the only thing that gave my life a meaning and has remained the crystal truth for me.

To protect the love I felt and imagined inside, without swapping it for the one offered to me on the outside, I had to use a great deal of care and inventiveness. First, I had to hide away that clean sacred love deep in my heart, and construct there a small secret stash that no one but I would be able to find. That way I could be sure that my love would remain unharmed; no one would take it away from me or destroy it. It would be safe there, and hence I would be, too, and if I hid my crystal-clear true love, I would also save myself. This worked. For example, when I was very little, I could not stay away from my mom. Every separation from her was a complete tragedy for me. Also, when we quarreled and she would tell me something hurtful or would turn away from me, I thought that my world was over for the rest of eternity and there would never be any love in it again. I remember that those arguments and my feelings of loss would simply break my heart into little pieces.

But then, as some time passed, it was okay and I would calm down and forget. After a while I even learned not to pay attention to those hurtful words, not to take them to heart, so to speak. So, what happened? Did I grow up, get used to it, became stronger and more enduring? No. I simply hid away my love, my sacred essence deeply in my heart and locked it with a key. At the same time, I could still feel and experience emotions; and my heart was still beating. But my main source of strength and truth was now inside and safe, and that gave me confidence in the future, some sort of a feeling of control and stability. I was doing my best to stay connected with this source of love, I was afraid of forgetting it. I believed that one day it would be full of life once again. My imagination was the connection between my loving heart and my mind. In it, I imagined myself surrounded with love in all its manifestations.

As I got a little older, I began to draw, in my imagination, romantic pictures about love. Like fairytales and myths, I imagined a prince who would save me and open up the love in me. I watched romantic movies, cried and dreamed; I read books about love stories. And each time my heart would remind me that there is a beautiful treasure, hidden deep inside and that one day I would definitely find it.

Yet, with time, I did forget where I hid the treasure and the fact that this once-beautiful, unconditional love was already inside me, flowing freely and naturally. So, I began to look for it in the outside world. I was simply obsessed with this search. I needed to be loved by everyone without exception: parents, teachers, boys, girls, best friends, and random people who played no particular role in my life. I put forth every effort to earn that love, make an impression, be well-liked—in a word, I did everything so that everyone would fall in love with me at first sight. It truly was not enough for me to be just liked; I wanted to be really loved, truly and deeply. And to get there, I was willing to change my inner form however necessary, as long as it fit the other person and he would finally give me the love, of which I had been dreaming so much.

Meanwhile, two processes started to take place inside me. One was the result of me actually finding the love outside. The other happened each time people would push me away or remain indifferent to me.

I will start with the first. It so happened that I began to feel boys' attention toward me at a fairly young age. Maybe they perceived my need to make them fall in love with me and gave into it; or maybe my blind faith in the force of love resonated in their hearts. One way or another, many boys at our school were in love with me. What is curious is that it did not fill me; it did not even please me. On the contrary, I constantly felt that it was something wrong. It was not the love that I was seeking. It did not warm my heart. As a result, throughout all my school years, I did not have any romantic relationships, only unsuccessful attempts. At the same time, I felt very empathic toward the boys who were in love with me; I pitied them and tried to cheer them up and even would find another love for them. Yet, I myself would continue to search tirelessly.

Another scenario also existed—when no one would love me at all. I felt that especially with my school teachers. Many of them simply could not stand me and humiliated me in every way possible. I remember very clearly the feeling when my heart would shrink into a tight ball and, as if covered by a layer of icy crust, would freeze inside. And the more cruelty, indifference, and simple lack of love I felt around me, the colder my heart became. I was still vulnerable and sensitive. I simply stopped showing my vulnerability and sensitivity—they were hidden deep in my heart, too, locked away, and surrounded by a wall of ice.

Interestingly, on the surface, I showed "love" openly. I could hug someone easily and tell him I loved him (or her). These words, that once were so sacred and pure to me, gradually stopped having such a profound meaning. That is, on the surface, I was a very "loving" person and I cannot say that this love was fake. Unfortunately, it was just a pitiful attempt at the love that was stored inside me. Yet, without having gone through the entire journey and losing faith, I would not have been able to remember the path back to my heart.

I had a few serious and long relationships during my college years and I even had a big dramatic first love story that would have made a good movie. But only when I met my future husband, did my heart begin to open and trust again. It was not about something that he did or said to me. It was the way he loved me, the way his heart touched mine. It just felt true, vulnerable and safe at the same time. I was able to finally look inside myself and discover my heart again. Of course, first I had to thaw the ice around it, and the presence of my husband and then children helped me enormously in doing so. I know for sure that they came into my life not because of endless search on the outside, but rather as a reward for my persistence and faith in love in all its manifestations. Thanks to their warmth and love, as well as my inner search that heated my heart, the ice finally melted, and that sacred stream of unconditional, healing love began to bubble up once again.

Now, when I am writing these words, I feel inside how warm and open my heart is and how much love there is in it—not the kind of love that screams, calls, or saves, but the one that is calm, unconditional, and true. In my life, even now there are events and encounters that make my heart cringe, close, or freeze to protect itself. But now I trust that my heart is strong enough to be open and vulnerable. Everything that happens in my heart is very important to me and that is why I treat it with great attentiveness, care, respect, and love.

Here my Inner Heart Companion shares the message that comes straight from my heart:

I know that I have an unlimited source of unconditional love that will heal any wounds and I trust that my heart becomes only stronger from every experience that I feel openly. In return to my trust, my heart keeps warm the rooms of my Inner Home that need the heat, sending the first responder of the healing and magical love where it is needed most. I can feel physically that the waves of my love are becoming bigger and wider and spreading far beyond my limits. I believe that such love has no boundaries and it can perform real miracles. And I am aware that while it flows in my Inner Home freely and naturally, my life goes on fully.

On the Way to
My Playfulness and Curiosity

When I was little, I did not have a chance to play enough. The life around me was so very serious. So I, too, wanted to become serious, grown-up, and a know-it-all. Although, I do remember myself playing a lot with my imagination and creating different magical realms. Years later I realized how powerful my imagination is and the great role playfulness has in my life.

Playing a game (and I mean a spontaneous, imaginary game) supposes an element of the unknown, of curiosity, of enjoying the process—without caring about the result. When you start to play, you have no idea where it will take you and how it will end. This is what the real readiness for adventure and discovery, bravery, and even risk means. Most importantly, while playing, you live in the present moment while being completely consumed and enchanted by the magic of your own imagination and the very process of the game. In this moment, you do not think about the past or plans for the future. You are completely present here-and-now—with your body, your mind, your soul, and your heart. It is as if everything inside you wakes up and comes to life, starts to sparkle, and is eager to come out. Everything becomes important, even the smallest details. Yet, when you are playing, everything is easy, natural, without an excessive seriousness, without effort and stress.

This playfulness also awakens true curiosity—like a child's free desire to take apart, look over in detail, and explore. It is precisely this curiosity that brings us to the greatest discoveries. It is not necessarily the passion or the desire to solve some mystery, but an effortless and playful inquisitiveness that allows one to enjoy the very process of exploring.

I think that had I played enough as a child, my life journey would have been less stressful and more full of joy. But it so happened that even when I played as a child, my games were serious, more suitable for adults. I was growing up with a feeling that life is not a game, but something serious, and I had to treat it as such. Maybe it saved me from certain silly mistakes or dangers. Yet, it was precisely this seriousness and lack of practice to play spontaneously that pressured me, depriving me of a flexibility in my thoughts, actions, and life decisions.

I remember that at the age of 16, I already felt myself such a hard, sturdy structure that knew ahead of time how everything should happen and when. I felt myself very adult and serious—an unmovable boulder. It seems in part that is why I had an escape plan in my mind to change everything in my life and go to live and study in Israel. It was the first seriously-unserious journey in my life that moved me and allowed me to awaken my curiosity and playfulness. Then, the elements of the playfulness began to appear in my life more and more. I was alone in a new country, facing many unknowns and feeling very vulnerable. Spontaneously, I started to play a role of someone who trusted herself, knowing in general where I was going and what I was looking for. You could say, it was pretense. Yes, maybe pretense, but not hypocrisy. I was not trying to lie to anyone, but rather to convince myself that I could be this way, that I could be credible in this new role in a new space—and it worked. The role emerged almost spontaneously and grew each day.

I remember that a couple of months after arriving at the school I attended, I gave a long and profound speech in Hebrew. Yet, I only knew a few words in Hebrew—I had written the speech ahead of time, translated it, and memorized it. But everyone around had a clear impression that I was fluent in Hebrew. So, everyone began to treat me in a way that left me no choice and I began to speak almost immediately, and without much effort. To this day I cannot recall clearly how it happened. I only remember that I myself started to believe that I was speaking Hebrew, and this game became my reality.

In a same playful and spontaneous way, I later became a journalist, and eventually wound up in the world of the cinema. I remember how, working with the actors, I was looking at them and thinking how lucky they were since they could be anyone they wanted to. They could take any role, practice and expand it, thereby developing their own inner repertoire. They could scream, get angry, love, or hate. They could express their most hidden emotions and feelings without hurting anyone; on the contrary, they were getting praise and recognition for it. I put forth every effort to help those actors to express their truth fully and spontaneously, because by then I had already believed in this incredible force residing in the ability to play fully and naturally.

I began to notice how people use this power of playfulness in various ways. Many adults perceive this gift differently than children, turning it into pretense, fake and affectedness. At a certain point in life, the difference between these two states—faking living and playing living—became obvious and clear to me. I no longer wanted to pretend, but rather play. I wanted to have the fullest experience of my life, believing sincerely and trusting the game, creating realities, feeling with my open heart, expressing feelings and emotions freely. I wanted to try new roles, new states and new ways of being. And to enjoy every minute of it, being curious and accepting the unknown.

When I had my son, and then my daughter, I was able to finally fulfill this missing part of my childhood with this kind of playing. Our favorites were the imaginary games. We would invent entire worlds, different characters, stories, and adventures. I was learning from my children to see the world through my imagination, when any stick can become a dragon or a wizard. I took seriously everything that they saw with their imagination and played in this world with them. This play created a special intimacy between us, like between companions, or travelers conquering new worlds. The act of play for my son has become as natural as breathing and years ago he actually became an actor when he was only 5 years old. My daughter is full of playfulness, imagination, and ability to create, no matter what she does.

Initially, it seemed to me that I was doing this for the kids, trying to give them what I did not have enough of in my childhood. But later I realized that I myself desperately needed to recapture this ability, because only through my imagination and the power of the playfulness I was able to free myself from that heavy weight of seriousness and responsibility that I was carrying since my childhood. This responsibility was to always do things right, perfectly, without making mistakes and asking for help. It was not a true responsibility for my actions, but a misguided perfectionism, which squelched my true nature.

So, with play I became much lighter, more flexible, and began to shine more. I wanted to expand my inner repertoire, without getting stuck in the same roles (an offended wife, a worrying mom, a career-focused woman, a crying little girl, etc.). The ability to play and express curiosity about myself, people around me and life itself, became a healing and inspiring gift to me. These expanded roles were the ones that brought me to my true purpose—not just to provide emotional assistance, but to support people discover themselves all over again, using psychodrama and other action methods. The way J.L. Moreno, the father of Psychodrama, described this process is that we simply take on a new role we desire or are interested in and play it (fully live it), until it becomes natural and true for us. Then, we are able to create our own rules, our unique and authentic way of playing this role and connect our personal true meaning to it.

I believe that too often a serious attitude toward life and ourselves prevents us from expressing our imagination, a sincere curiosity, playfulness, and the joy of the very process. We become hostages of our rehearsed and artificial roles, life scenarios and unnecessary beliefs. We are afraid to step beyond the boundaries of the adult, serious world in order to be silly, fantasize, play a new game, even for a while. We may even be afraid that we will not understand the rules of the new game. When I get stuck in this place, I remind myself to look how the children do it. They change the rules as they wish, come up with new ones, and enjoy themselves even if they do not completely understand the meaning of the game. They find joy in what they don´t know yet. They are free in their search and excited about every new imaginary role and enthralling game. They are curious and interested in life itself because to them it seems to be an incredible adventure, an endless beautiful game. I believe that adults, who were able to keep or newly discover this ability in themselves, are no longer afraid to live and establish what are considered as serious goals. Living with playfulness actually allows us to take serious steps with more resolve.

I sincerely believe that precisely this ability to play, imagine, and freely express dreams and curiosity can drive us to the most serious, profound, and important discoveries of our lives.

Message from my Inner Personal Assistant:

Your playfulness and curiosity have become strong inner powers. They allow you to keep your soul active, your mind flexible and your heart brave and adventurous. They help you to feel light even when you take serious steps. These powers give you an opportunity to accept the unknown and release the control. When you feel that life is too heavy or you are stuck, just step into your inner playground and release your playfulness. That will bring new energy, joy and light to your Inner Home.

On the Way to Finding My Own Answers

Let us imagine that in every person's Inner Home there is a vast library with many different books. Some are ancient, written in language we cannot fully understand. Some, conversely, are very clear and easy to process. Some are written as fairy-tales, giving us answers through metaphors and imagery. There are books that present practical guides to action. All these books are directly related to our life and knowledge we would like to discover. Each time we want an answer, locate information, or learn something, we can go to our inner library and find it. Most importantly, we know the answers will be most correct and true for us. However, sometimes such a search may take much time because first we need to find the correct book, then study it till we find the answer. Often, though, we are impatient and want to find everything quickly. So, while we have this treasure in our own home, we tend to look elsewhere, where we believe it will be faster and easier to find. We can, for example, ask someone and get their subjective opinion. We can use the general search system and find a universal answer there. We can look at how other people resolve similar issues and imitate them. Or, we can go with the flow, believing that somehow the answer will find us on its own.

All these options have a viable reason to exist in our lives. Under certain circumstances, they may prove very valuable and useful, sometimes even irreplaceable. But what to do with all that treasure of knowledge stored in our Inner Home? Will it remain unused and unappreciated? Nobody demands that we spend our days and nights in this library until we know every book intimately. Who could afford this? We have other things to do, responsibilities, and life processes beyond the limits of this library. We can visit the library periodically, looking at and getting used to this treasure. The more we visit, learning what the books have to offer, the better we will learn to orient ourselves. Then the search for the answers we need can become a true pleasure. It does not matter how original and unique the needed answers will be. The important thing is that we will know that we found them on our own, through our personal effort, patience, persistence, and curiosity. We will be sure of the legitimacy of these answers and their relevance to us because we found them in our own Inner Home, in our personal, unique inner library.

I have always loved to read and since an early age treated books with a special kind of respect and awe. In my life, I have read many books. There were times when I would read anything and everything I laid my eyes on. There were also times when I was looking for specific books and read what was truly important and valuable to me. Many of those books inspired, filled me, and made me think. In them I discovered new visions that drastically changed my thoughts and views. But after a while, I would forget what I had read. The only thing that truly remained inside me was what I felt when reading a certain book. Those feelings would start internal invisible processes that continued to resonate and influence me for a long time. I may forget very quickly the answer and information I receive, but I do remember the feeling of inspiration, glee, relief, awe, nervousness, curiosity, shock, and insight. These are the feelings I am looking for when opening a new book and listening to whether it will resonate in my heart. These feelings allow me to get closer to my own answers.

So, I learned over time to look for these answers in my Inner Home, in my inner, rich library. I started to direct the most important life questions inward. It is a simple process of talking myself through them precisely and truthfully, and patiently waiting for an answer. The answer would invariably come, at the right time and right place. Of course, such search for answers requires much more patience, persistence, curiosity, attention, and trust. But every such answer has been a true reward. The information that came to me from inside was always remarkably true, relevant, and applicable to my life. Most importantly, I would never lose this knowledge. It would become a part of me, my experience, my treasure, my life wisdom.

With time, the search for my inner answers became an habitual and natural activity. I navigate pretty well inside my inner library and often know exactly which book contains a particular answer. Although most of the time this process is unconscious and intuitive. I do not stress my brain as when reading some hard-to-understand literature or when trying to remember what it is that I have learned. On the contrary, it is as if I give my brain a chance to rest, to relax, all the while receiving a precise and valid answer.

My inner library is in constant demand, its space filling and expanding. I continue to read, listen to the opinion of others, search the Internet for information, and go with the flow. I continue to be inspired by feelings that are so generously given to me by people who share their personal real and imaginary stories. Only now I know for certain where my most important and true knowledge and answers lie. They do not need to be unique, perfect, or special. They are simply mine, and therein lie their value, truth, and depth.

The message from my Inner Housekeeper:

You have everything you need to know within you. All the true answers are there. Nobody can know the answer about you better than you. Just keep visiting your inner library and explore your inner knowledge, wisdom and imagination. If you have the question, you have the answer. This piece of information is waiting to show up for you. Just be patient and wait for the one that is true for you, that is coming from your Inner Home.

Filling My Inner Home
with Connections and Meaning

No matter what your destination is right now,
you are always on The Way Home.

On the Way to Being Meaningful

How difficult it is to uncover the meaning of one's own existence! It is especially hard when we try to discover it in relation to others. Productive discussions and exchange of knowledge and experience, as well as commonly-accepted judgments, are vital to life. Yet, I consider that a search for an individual meaning is exactly that—an exclusive and individual responsibility.

I sincerely believe that each of us is born with a specific purpose; that in each creation resides a profound and extremely important, exceptional meaning. Each of us plays an equally important role in the common-coordinate system of the Universe, that is to say, the system of universal balance and interconnection to each other. Each of us has been given by nature a chance to discover the meaning of our own existence and have a life full of purpose, value, and uniqueness. Each of us has a natural desire to answer this vitally important question for ourselves, "Who am I and what is my meaning, my purpose in this world?"

Of course, this question did not pass me by. While in childhood and adolescence I thought of it as an insuperable and unsolvable problem. However, over the course of my life, as I gained simple, yet important knowledge, I have found that each problem, as unresolvable and unrealistic as it may seem, must be simplified. To clarify, *the solution to the problem* must be simplified, not its importance. It becomes obvious that if so many people in this world have already asked this question about a meaningful existence, then this question is meaningful. As a result, if it is a meaningful question, there must be a meaningful answer. Based on my life experience, I can say that the very desire to ask a question that we believe is important and legitimate, opens our search system. It is then that we begin to receive varied information both from outside and within that is directly related to our question. Then comes an important moment that can take our search into different directions. It is the moment that transitions this natural and universally important question into a philosophical, theoretical, hypothetical realm, that is complex and incomprehensible and, maybe, unrealistic. Or, perhaps it turns our question into a simple, everyday and natural curiosity that has very specific live answers.

So, at this juncture, we now have a choice and it is driven by whether we are ready to accept the responsibilities that life imposes on us, that are meant to uncover our own unique meaning to ourselves and the people around us. We are by no means talking about sacrificing ourselves in the name of a greater purpose. We are talking about our conscious choice— not in favor of comfort and a lack of desire to learn, but in favor of discoveries, challenges, experiences, new circumstances and opportunities that life offers to us and that open us.

That is, do we really want to hear a truthful answer to this question, or at least get some new information to consider? Or do we only pretend that we are interested, while in reality we choose to remain deaf and indifferent to our own meaning in this world?

By being truly open and curious about purpose and importance in my life journey, I adjust my personal soul navigator, making it even more precise and pointing in the direction of the meaning of my entire being. The more present I am to the circumstances life offers me, going through them thoughtfully, the stronger my soul navigator is, and the clearer the deep and unique meaning in me is manifested. Through accepting and comprehending my life experience (whether in the process or by looking back), the mystery of my purpose becomes more visible. I do not need to understand what is behind the mysterious circumstances that life offers me. I just need to go through them, being as present and open as I can in everything that happens to me, simply because I cannot control what life presents to me. I can only choose the way I respond to it. So instead of running away, evading, complaining, victimizing myself, and pretending to be blind, led by someone else, I can accept and recognize this experience as another step toward understanding my purpose and unique meaning.

As soon as I transformed this significant question into my simple, everyday reality, a multitude of interesting discoveries began to pour out. The process was such: Each day I simply asked myself what my inner meaning or purpose was. I did not expect to hear the answer or to receive some kind of clarification. I was simply focused on this question and present with what life offered me that day. The answers that came were varied: Maybe I needed to be quiet, or I had to tell someone something important; maybe I should spend my time doing the house chores, or perhaps I needed to focus only on my work; maybe my purpose today is to pay extra attention to my children; or maybe I should create a bit of distance and dedicate my time to myself, allowing my children to have their personal space.

So, this daily exercise continues. As soon as I voice this question to myself about my own meaning for that day, the circumstances around me immediately begin to form a pattern that very clearly indicates which experience is the most important and precise for me. It does not mean, however, that I devote myself entirely to what life throws at me, without taking the initiative. Sometimes, I even resist and get very upset if things do not go my way. At times, it is completely unclear to me what my purpose is for the day. But over time, I have learned to trust life and believe that I am filled with meaning and purpose every day, independently of what happens to me. I think it is this very faith that helps me go through each life experience, however difficult or simple, with meaning and a greater value in my life. Every such experience, like a bead, is strung on the life thread to form a beautiful necklace.

Looking back, I can clearly see how each of those circumstances and responsibilities that I lived through, ones that once seemed insignificant and distracting from the greater meaning, have brought me to today's purpose. All I had to do was to accept them as a given and acknowledge their significance, even if I did not clearly understand why they were significant. Then, the meaning of that experience would begin to manifest itself, like some pictures that only appear in light and warmth. Today, I look at these pictures and say to myself, "Oh, so, that is what is it was; that is the meaning it had." I am not able to see the whole story because I am but a tiny particle in this huge and complex picture of life. But I am an important particle, filled with a very specific meaning. And the more responsible and honest I will be about expressing my own meaning and significance, the brighter and clearer will the overall picture be.

"What *is* the purpose, the meaning of my being?", one can spend years mulling over and even tortured by this important question and not find the courage to accept the answer and, therefore, not get any closer to understanding it. On the other hand, one can simply accept this mysterious purpose as the main rule of playing the game of life and calmly wait for clues and answers. And what is more important, to trust that there is always a meaning, that this is our choice to bring this meaning into our everyday life. All that is required of us is an attentive participation in this profound composition, following the rules honestly, openly, and consciously. It is then that our Inner Home will be filled with everyday meaning, significance, and fulfillment.

A message from my Inner Heart Companion:

Today, I feel that my inner meaning is to be as true as I can be at this moment. It is not about showing truth, it is about being true. Not showing meaning, but by being meaningful. I do not need to make any extra effort in order to be meaningful, because I already am, from the very start. I just need to allow my inner meaning appear in my everyday life, to accept its presence and to be attentive to its signals. Without overthinking, analyzing or fantasizing, I can simply trust with all my heart that there is always meaning in me. Every minute of my life I am full of meaning and purpose. When I am true and present, I can recognize it and follow its growth and expansion.

On the Way to my True Light

During many years, I unconsciously avoided the topic of inner light and did not attempt to dig into the truth in these questions: What is the nature of my inner light? What influences it and how? Nevertheless, these questions, in different forms, were coming up increasingly during my sessions with clients or workshops, in which I participated or led myself. It was very difficult for me to come closer to this topic within myself; for some reason, it felt too intimate and even unsafe. I sensed that in this area I could discover some very strong feelings and emotions, such as shame, lack of safety, vulnerability, and tenderness. At some point, I began to observe and explore this topic through the examples of other people—from a safe distance, so to speak, as a neutral observer.

Many different stories seemed to tell that when emotional trauma happened, the person had had an experience of being completely filled with light and was able to let it out freely, without trying to hide or protect it. These people often described the violence toward their most vulnerable, intimate, and pure expressions. People who had survived sexual abuse related that it was precisely on those days they were filled with a feeling of beauty, happiness, and light, especially in the cases of very young victims.

Listening to these stories, I suddenly, and very clearly, saw the following picture. The light that flows freely from one person blinds another, who has long since lost his own source of light and now lives in a complete and impenetrable inner darkness. So, this other person feels a burning desire to take this light away, appropriate it, or at the very least turn it off, pull the plug, cut all the wires—do something so that this light will finally stop blinding him/her, who already can barely see clearly. This image completely shocked me. I looked around even more and began to observe the relationships between parents and children in everyday situations. I witnessed such instances as these many times: parents screaming at their kids, offending them, and at times even humiliating them is precisely when the children are in their most pure and beautiful state. For example, when they laugh heartily or play with all their soul, not noticing anything around; or slow down to admire a leaf flying by; or stop to feel the wind with a happy and peaceful smile on their face. It is in those moments that some of the parents begin to yell at their children, getting angry with them for not answering immediately. Or they jerk the child around, saying mean and hurtful things, like: "Wake up already!"; "You don't care for anyone, beside yourself."; "Stop dreaming."; "Grow up already."; "Can't you just be normal, behave well, do what's expected from you?!?" And so on. I found that many adults become physically and emotionally aggressive exactly in moments like these.

Therefore, I began paying more attention to myself and noticed that sometimes I am afraid of how bright and pure the light is that comes from my own children—and most importantly, how freely and openly it flows. I discovered that along with happiness and love for my children, I sometimes feel scared, seeing how unprotected and vulnerable they are, precisely because they do not hide this light and share it openly and fearlessly with those around.

Gradually, I was able to go more deeply into myself and hear my own story about my relationship with my inner light. For many years, I was living with a feeling that someone is constantly cutting it off, blocking it with his shadow, breaking it as soon as I let it out. Even when I was alone, I often felt as though storm clouds were filling the sky and everything inside would turn opaque and gloomy—and sometimes even completely dark. Moreover, I often stopped perceiving this inner light flowing freely within myself. I envisioned it as merely the proverbial 'light at the end of the tunnel' that one tries with all her strength to reach, without losing hope and faith that someday she will achieve that. I also recalled a time from my youth when the trusted adults would interrupt me half-sentence (that very important sentence that so desperately needed to be said); how harsh their reaction sometimes was to my vulnerability, and how they tried forcibly to stop the pure and tender expressions of my soul. But most importantly, I discovered that I myself still keep putting out my inner light, 'with my own hands'. Sometimes I block it with the phrases and reactions that I received a long time ago and that still keep circling in my head. Sometimes, it is my own gloomy and dark thoughts that apparently want to warn me, but in reality, they simply try to kill the manifestation of the most wonderful vulnerability of my soul, where all the most beautiful that exists in me resides. I discovered that, instead of focusing on defending myself against any external enemies, criticism, violence or manipulations, I should pay more attention to what I keep doing within, as a bad habit, on autopilot. I need to pay attention to which inner mechanisms, set in motion by someone a long time ago, are still blocking my inner light from me. I began to follow and track my own thoughts, my inner reactions, and my attitude toward myself that transpired in different situations. I started to imagine my own clear light, flowing freely, its power and purpose for me. It became of utmost importance to me to stop any attempts on my part to limit the flow of this light within me. I was no longer able to live without it, to remain in my own shadow, while knowing how bright I could be. I became the guardian of my own inner light, and realized that only I, and no one else, am responsible for that light within me. Only I can put it out or turn it on again.

My inner light is me—the *me* that was originally intended. It is the spark from which I came and that turned into a warm and strong flame. My light is my true *me*, without restrictions and definitions. It is something that no one can take away from me, just as no one can give it to me. People around me can throw a shadow on my light, but it is my decision, and mine alone, whether to remain in that shadow or turn toward the light again. People I meet throughout my journey can illuminate me with their light, inspire, enlighten my inner universe, share their life experiences and paths they had taken toward their inner light. But nobody can give that light to me or discover it in me. Only I can make that inner choice, sometimes with an extra effort to give it a chance to flow through me openly and freely, as was intended by nature. Yet, it is not a choice that I make once and for all. It is a constant inner practice—a practice of life. It is a positive choice in favor of my light, and not a fear or denial of darkness. I cannot avoid a dark time of the day, just as it is impossible to be constantly in a naturally lit space. I am no longer afraid of my own darkness precisely because I am not afraid of losing my light. I believe that after every night, a new day will come, and from the clouds the sun will shine.

My light continually grows and illuminates my inner space; it is my inner strength and my power. It comes from my very core, from the soft, vulnerable, and pure space of my soul. I no longer need to hide and protect it. Because today, my light protects me and in its natural, tender and free glow, I feel myself truly at home.

On the Way to
My True Connections

I know and trust that all people on Earth are interconnected. These invisible threads between us spread much farther than we can imagine. I do not need to maintain them artificially or deliberately create them. They exist whether I want them to or not. The most important thing for me on this journey is simply to notice these connections and relationships. This simple act of careful observation brings them from the dusky shadows, making them visible to my heart and full of my own meaning.

I attentively watch the people, whom I connect to on my way, no matter if I meet them in-person, read their book, hear their thoughts, or share with them a particular life experience. From the start, each person merits my respect and attention—simply because I respect human nature and strongly believe in the best and the purest aspects that will inevitably show in every person. At the same time, I try to separate and clarify the simple (pleasant or unpleasant) interactions from connections that bring me true meaning, recognizing those who share my path at the moment. Making this distinction is important, because if I were to maintain a relationship with each person I meet on my way, follow the social rituals accepted in today's society, I simply would not have time and energy for relationships with people who are truly important to me, for the connection to myself. If I find myself constantly chasing interactions, friendships, and maintaining all the contacts created in the name of socialization itself, there is no truth for me in it—only an illusion of a connection with this world. But if I treat my connection with people as a natural one that already exists in a true form, I have no need to create anything artificially.

Therefore, it is essential for me to trust and be open to the fact that those connections that are important and true for me will inevitably appear in my life. And, they really do appear, especially when I am truly connected with myself, with my inner universe. When this connection with my truth, my nature, my needs, my Inner Home is strong, I am available to look around and see with whom I already have, or am beginning to build, a similar true connection. Such connection can show itself in various forms. For example, it is the people with whom I can be real, showing my true nature, my needs; with whom I feel at Home, safe and natural; someone who grows and changes together with me, thus allowing me to live in the present. More importantly, it is someone whom I can trust to let into my Inner Home and know that he or she will be careful enough to not destroy anything. I can also feel a true meaningful connection with someone who takes me back into my childhood home, stirring in me the long-forgotten memories and sensations, or even reflecting my traumatic experiences. Often, it is such relationships that help me untie the invisible knots of my past and get closer to the Home where I want to live and grow today. Although, with this kind of relationship it is important to realize that sometimes, if not trained and careful, they may ruin and re-traumatize my whole being. If that happened, I grow apart from those people.

Sometimes it seems it is very difficult to sort out this endless flow of people and recognize the most valuable and true connections for me. But as soon as I relax and trust the cosmic and wise net, without trying to control or artificially create relationships, all that was hidden suddenly comes to light. At that point, all I must do is simply observe, listen to my heart, and heed the uncovered truth.

I sincerely believe that in everyone's life there is at least one person with whom a connection is true and filled with a special meaning and value. It is this precise moment, when I have at least one person like this in my life and I allow our relationship to fully blossom, that I feel a connection with all the people on the planet. It is then that my relationship with the world becomes true and genuine, because when I am truly connected with one person, I am connected with the entire world.

One can run from these most genuine and truthful relationships, just as at times we try to run away from ourselves, from our Inner Home. We can trade these relationships for many others, maintaining the status of a very outgoing and socially active person.

But we can also recognize their value and accept this simple and true order. First, we connect with ourselves, then with those who are welcomed in our Inner Home, then with those around us, and then with the whole world.

My Inner Heart Companion speaks this message:

In my life today, people with whom I am connected by these true, visible, manifested relationships are not so many (although not too few either). Each of these connections contains a huge world, an endless universe. I cannot even put into words how important and valuable each is for me. These people, who are so close, are in the living room of my Inner Home. There they feel comfortable and at ease. Each lives inside me, regardless of the physical distance or the frequency of our interaction. These people in my life are not passersby or guests. They form a part of that closest circle that becomes the reflection of my living journey and experience—just as I become the same for them. Each is also an invariable and irreplaceable part of my inner social atom. They fill my inner living room with laughter, tears, emotions, discussions and excited interactions, most diverse sincere feelings, and enormous love—with life itself. I am not attached to these people but am truly connected to them.

On the Way to
Letting My Ego and
Ambitions Rest in Peace

Since I was little, I constantly heard the word "egoist" and "selfish", which to me always carried a negative connotation. Often, when I wanted to do something for myself or in my own way that would go against the desires of the rest of my family, I would be called an egoist. Thus, from a young age, I learned that being selfish is bad and tried very hard not to break the unspoken code of conduct, as to not become a selfish person in the eyes of the others.

On the other hand, my surrounding environment was imbued with ambitions and, at a very early age I, too, was taken with those ambitious desires. In the setting in which I grew up, being ambitious was considered good, even prestigious. According to the common opinion, it had nothing to do with egoism or self-interest; on the contrary, it would present one as a complete and active member of society. So, for a very long time, I had been trapped between those two contradictions and could not free myself from their pressure. It looked as though, on the one hand, in order for me to become an accomplished individual in life, I had to constantly think about myself, my advancement and growth, my goals, my career, and stop at nothing in following my own ambitions. I say "ambitions" and not "wishes" precisely because choosing my true wishes and desires was selfish and, hence, inappropriate. On the other hand, I was so afraid of having a reputation as a selfish, ego-centered person that I was willing to give up any of my true needs and desires. This was a very convoluted and tight knot that took me many years to untangle. As a desire to share this process with you, in my mind was born a tale about two brothers.

Once upon a time, there were twin brothers. One was called Creation and the other, Ego—such unusual names. They were closely connected in the way that only twins can be. They influenced and felt one another. At times, they did not even know who had begun a thought, and who had finished it; who made the first step, and who joined in. Those two little, very-similar boys lived together and shared their misfortunes and happiness equally. Day-by-day, they lived and grew into who they were meant to be.

Creation was growing up a sweet, quiet, calm boy who did not insist on anything. Ego, on the other hand, was very pushy, screaming, assertive, and always fought for everything— even those things he did not truly need. The louder, more active and assertive was Ego, the quieter and more unassuming was Creation. As a result, Creation received almost no attention from others; he was not being taken seriously even by his own family. Ego could not accept that his brother was so weak, spineless, and nearly unnoticeable (at least as he appeared to him), and constantly fought to defend his rights. He screamed, insisted, even threatened while trying to take from life what, in his view, rightfully belonged to Creation. Ego got so carried away with this endless fight for justice that he no longer paid attention to himself and his attitude. To him, it seemed that he himself did not even need anything anymore; what he needed was for others to acknowledge his brother Creation, for them to take him seriously.

At the same time, Creation remained absolutely imperturbable and at times appeared to not pay the slightest attention to Ego's efforts. He liked his quiet silence, and invisibility, even avoiding his brother who constantly wanted something from him. At some point, the brothers grew far apart and almost did not notice each other any longer. That was the moment when their father, Observer, intervened. He decided to speak with his sons.

"What do you want, Ego?" he asked one of the brothers.

"I want my brother to be taken seriously, to be appreciated, respected. I want others to listen to him, to know what he is capable of. I am willing to spend my entire life to prove that my brother deserves attention, that he is valuable, and should be treated accordingly."

"And what do you want, Creation?", the father asked his other son.

"I simply want to be quiet and calm. I want others not to distract me from my peace and not meddle with my way to living."

At hearing this, Ego became indignant.

"Can you not understand," he yelled to his brother, "that I am fighting for *you*? I, too, could simply rest and enjoy the silence, like you. Do you think I do not want that? But instead, I am fighting for your honor, sacrificing myself!"

"But I never asked you for it," said Creation, surprised.

"That's the problem. You never ask for anything and never insist on anything. Do you really think that I would simply stand there and watch you waste all your potential? I had to take control of our lives. If you were just a little bit more active, talked about your wishes just a bit louder and clearer, I would not have had to fight for both of us."

"In other words, my silence prevented you from being quiet and calm?", said Creation, even more astonished.

"I don't know," said Ego, exhausted. "All I know is that I am tired of this fighting. I do not even remember what I wanted to achieve. It just seemed to me that everyone around me was expecting something of me, that so many hopes were put in me; that I had to act, had to be strong and in the center. Remember, how when we were little, you would whisper to me your wishes and dreams? I wanted with all my heart for them to come true for you. But you did absolutely nothing for it to happen. What was I to do? I could not allow our lives to go to waste."

"Forgive me," said Creation, softly. "You are right, I seem to have been far away. I was only enjoying the silence and invisibility, cherishing my dreams, but not wanting to share them openly. Maybe I was scared, maybe I even felt my uselessness. It does not matter. What is important is that I no longer want to hide in the shadows from life and put the responsibility for my existence onto you. I am ready to act, but I am not going to fight anyone or try to prove anything. I will express myself in the way that is true for me, I will share what is valuable and precious to me. This way, I will still be able to enjoy my peace and, at the same time, express myself openly, being fully present in my own life. I will make my dreams come true and hope that they will bring happiness to someone else too."

"But what about me?", asked Ego, stunned.

"You will finally be able to rest and stop fighting on my behalf. Maybe you will even be able to enjoy the peace and quiet and hear your own desires."

"Will you be able to handle it without me?" Ego asked with a smile.

"We will always be together, no matter what. We are twin brothers. We feel and share our strengths with each other. That is why, if I ever have to fight for anything, I am sure you will come to help me."

Since then, Ego has become much quieter and calmer. He is often silent and spends more time observing his brother Creation, although if he sees any injustice or lie, he immediately jumps up and runs to bring order. Creation, on the hand, leads a very active life, filled with purpose, all the while keeping his silence, but not being afraid of his own voice.

Returning to my story, today I can easily imagine that in my inner universe exists a special corner where my ego now relaxes, basking in sunlight. My ego has not been fired as unnecessary, or sent into exile; instead, it is on an unlimited and well-deserved vacation. It is surrounded by friends, ambitions, celebrating life, and is not in a rush. It is calmly watching over Creation that is blossoming in my inner universe and opening up to the outside world. My ego can finally enjoy peace and quiet because I heard its pain and fatigue and let it rest by my assuming the responsibility for life and development of my true potential.

When my true self, my creative potential, my inner universe emerges and opens up, I no longer need any efforts of my ego. In its struggle, it only pushes me away from the world, does not allow me to grow and show my true value. When my ego accepts that I do not need it to fight, it becomes quiet and calm. I can then hear my true dreams and desires. I can hear the soft voice of creation, and not the scream of my ego mixed with a noisy chorus of my ambitions.

The message my Inner Heart Companion shares:

Today, I can openly express my true ideas, dreams and desires, without considering myself an egoist and at the same time without trying to make those dreams come true at any cost. I no longer have to worry about how the others will receive my creativity because now I know that both Ego and Creation are working together.

Expanding My Inner Home: Creating Gardens, Connecting with the Heavens

No matter what your destination is right now,
you are always on The Way Home.

On the Way to Overcoming My Inner Walls

I grew up with a very strong perception of external boundaries. At home, I clearly knew the boundaries I was not supposed to cross, and I never tried to do so. Yet, I cannot say that my parents were strict. Rather, on the contrary, I was allowed many things, even those that were forbidden to the other children. I felt reasonably free within those boundaries. I can say that in many aspects my parents were very lenient, even liberal, and I am extremely grateful to them for that. Their leniency taught me personal responsibility. Since I felt that my parents trusted me, I learned to trust myself in many areas, too. My parents seemed very sensible in establishing those boundaries that they did, and that gave me a feeling of clarity, protection and common sense.

Yet, as the years passed, I found out that besides the boundaries that still are natural and true for me, I have these inner walls that limit my vision and separate me from my truth, from the growth and expansion of my Inner Home. So, I asked myself: "How can it be that sometimes a protective boundary becomes a limitation? How do boundaries lose their positive and important quality and turn into obstacles—a wall around one's self?"

222

I recall one occasion when I was six or seven years-old. My mom and I were outside on a playground. As I was playing and climbing on various attractions, I remember that my mom said something to me, and I fired at her, "What?! Are you, crazy?" I immediately stopped talking because I realized that I had just crossed an important boundary, some red line. I can still see clearly the expression on my mother's face and a horrible feeling of guilt remains with me, even though I had meant nothing bad. That phrase had seemed to escape on its own. I realized instantly that I had hurt my mom's feelings and I promised myself that I would never let my words fly out freely like this again. I realized that I must pay very close attention to what I say because my words have a special meaning for her. Since my mother was my whole world, I transferred that boundary with absolute certainty onto the rest of the world. It was then that a filter in my head began working—no matter the day, the situation, or the people around me. It became a difficult task for me to speak my thoughts out loud, openly express my opinion, or be free with my words. So it was, in just one moment such an important protective boundary as a careful approach to my words and other people's feelings had transformed into a wall, a restriction, a limitation that stayed within me for years. I want to stipulate right now, though, that I see no fault on my mother's part in this. In the same way, I do not believe that parents should stop establishing boundaries for their children, out of fear of limiting them.

But I am equally certain that every person should have the right to question the established protective boundaries; check their relevance from time to time; relax or strengthen them, and rein them in or expand them before they turn into rigid walls. There are areas in our inner and outside space where boundaries are absolutely necessary, and if we lose them we can descend into chaos. Similarly, there are rooms inside us that are ready to grow and expand, that become too small for us, like a small pair of shoes that squeeze our feet from all angles. So, if we let ourselves question our own boundaries (that with time may turn into defenses), study them with attention and curiosity, we will allow ourselves to live freely, protecting but not limiting ourselves.

When I realized that these solid inner walls that I was working so hard to overcome are my own borders, I began to treat my boundaries with great care. This applies to the boundaries of my body, my personal space, and most importantly, my inner world. My attentiveness is about watching over them with love and care; observing and making conclusions, without relying on the commonly accepted definitions of the boundaries instead of the ones that are just and true for me in the here-and-now. I know that some of the boundaries that were instilled as a child are protecting me today, but still may turn into obstacles on the way to my inner growth and expansion.

I look closely at my inner borders and sometimes carefully and gently check if they are ready to be moved or transformed. But I do so ever so tenderly because I know that if I push hard, I will be forcing them—just like in a war, when the borders between the countries get erased under the pressure of the force. I am not trying to invade or take over other territories that do not belong to me yet, or to push myself where it may still be dark and even dangerous. I only expand the boundaries of my inner world in the directions that are illuminated, where the light reaches; where my personality is ready to be expressed. These new, unexplored spaces inside me are not an enemy territory, into which I force my way trying to confirm my own courage. This space that I can see beyond my inner walls, should excite and call me; it may be unfamiliar, but it feels welcoming, safe and natural.

It took me time to discover that my inner walls can come from my own boundaries that once served me well. And this is my responsibility only to revise my inner territory and check on the relevancy of those boundaries, to help myself expand my inner walls and inner space, while keeping it safe and natural. It is my great honor to take care of my Inner Home and to liberate it from unnecessary and irrelevant restrictions and limitations, to allow its constant growth and expansion.

Concerning these inner boundaries, I receive a message from my Inner Personal Assistant:

Your strength is to recognize what serves you in the present, what is helpful for you, and what keeps you in the past. You know that everything is transformable within you; there is nothing that cannot be moved or reconstructed for the sake of your own growth. When you are intent to live in the present and choose inner freedom over restrictions, your Inner Home will constantly continue to grow and expand.

On the Way to
Natural Spontaneity
and Creativity

I will begin with a clear and important saying from J. L. Moreno, the founder of Psychodrama, a psychotherapy method that discovered the power and value of spontaneity and creativity. "[Spontaneity is] an adequate response to a new situation and/or a novel response to an old situation." It is not what we usually think spontaneity is—an impulsive action. Moreno also believed that the divine act of Creation is not complete, that the Higher Power (God) that once created the universe and the cosmos, continues to create even now. A man, as Moreno called him, is a carrier of a Divine Spark, the energy that cannot be accumulated; it manifests itself only "here and now", in action. Moreno called this energy "creativity, art, or co-creation", referring to the belief that every one of us is a co-creator together with the Higher Power/God.

Only when I began to study and practice psychodrama, I discovered how creative and spontaneous I really am. I remembered all my childhood feelings, in which this perception of co-creation was present literally in every instant. Like all children, I reacted very quickly to new circumstances, expressed new spontaneous responses to the old situations, and very strongly perceived the presence of this divine energy that is born here-and-now. The older I got, the more I found myself under the influence—and sometimes, even under the pressure—of accepted behavior norms, laws, and canons. I wanted to please, to fit, to meet the expectations placed in me. Therefore, I acted and reacted increasingly on autopilot, clutching and holding back my own spontaneous, live expressions.

It was this clutching and holding back, and not my lack of ability to be spontaneous and creative, that had become the reason of my sometimes-inadequate reactions to new situations. That is, the more I held back what once came naturally and freely to me and was a part of the divine creative process (which can so often be seen in little children), the more inadequate were my spontaneous reactions, bursting out chaotically and uncontrollably. This proved to me even further that I should not show any spontaneity, which most often was expressed as impulsiveness or excessive emotionality. To the contrary, I learned to act based on accepted habits and norms. Back then I did not know that any creation and a true life begin with spontaneous chaos that gradually gains a shape, having its own logic, boundaries, balance, and harmony.

In such autopilot mode, it is very difficult to change, try new things, grow, and show flexibility, courage, and creativity. Moreno conducted research and showed scientifically that the lower our level of creativity, the higher the level of our fears and inner panic. And vice versa. The cycle becomes complicated and very difficult to break.

The journey of regaining my spontaneity and the feeling of co-creation was, just like all important processes, very gradual, consisting of small steps. I remember that, starting in my adolescence, I allowed myself to make decisions that were dictated solely by my intuition (that divine spark) and were not based on any rational explanation. Some of those decisions were not very reasonable, but I defended their adequacy and fought with all my strength for their existence. You could say, it was probably the youthful stubbornness, but this was the way my spontaneity and creativity were coming into the light. For me, it was vital to express new reactions (at least occasionally), and to act in the spur of the moment without thinking about the consequences.

Of course, this spontaneity was inadequate— or, as Moreno calls it, pathological spontaneity, just for the sake of the act. Yet, this very act was helping me warm up and get closer to my live, non-automated state. Thanks to such follies, my spontaneity would flicker, wake up, and I would discover courage, liveliness, flexibility, and the joy of life in me. With time, I noticed that many of my reactions, actions, and decisions born in the here-and-now, that is, in the moment, proved not only true, but also life-changing. I accepted the marriage proposal from my now-husband just after one-and-a-half months of knowing each other. In the same spontaneous way, my children were born. I chose my profession, which became one of the main purposes in my life, after having a dream, and so forth. These decisions were made impulsively and I can say that I was lucky that they were the right decisions. This was still not a true, conscious spontaneity—only its seeds. Yet, they were the first and most important steps toward my creativity, spontaneity, and co-creation.

When I began to study psychodrama as a tool that opens the healing and powerful force of spontaneity, my life filled with a wonderful and conscious experience. I was no longer afraid of changes; every day brought me so many extraordinary surprises and, at times, even true miracles. I began to live by the truth of my heart. That is, I relied on my feelings and not on the stories that my brain spat out like old songs. Most importantly, I learned to improvise. I no longer needed to think through, calculate, and prepare myself for every new step in my life. No matter how hard we try to plan and control everything, in reality things do not happen the way we expect, but sometimes they happen the way we cannot even imagine. I now know that when I find myself in a certain situation, this entire experience, knowledge, and my warmed-up, trained spontaneity inside me will turn on, and I will be able to live that moment easily and openly.

Spontaneity gives me the freedom of not being trapped by my thought-through plan (however 'genius' it may be); rather, it allows me to be sure of my ability to improvise, while enjoying the divine spark of the moment. It does not mean that I do not plan anything or establish goals; on the contrary, I enjoy organizing my life. The difference is that now I watch my reactions with great attention. I become aware of those that are automatic and memorized from the past that constantly try to impose on my present, and I don't choose them. I carefully listen to the voice that challenges and changes me and pushes me toward new adventures, discoveries, and growth. It is the voice that believes in my divine spark and does not look for conservation and, therefore stagnation, but rather turns every moment into a true creation. It is not a disconnect from life, not a process of an artificial creation of life, but a co-creation with the Highest Creator of our universe.

The result of this co-creation, which is a live and adequate reaction to my present, was the recovery of my creativity. Moreno defined creativity as an "arch substance" for a constructive expression of spontaneity; that is, a specific form for expressing of the real me in this particular moment. If we imagine the spontaneity as seeds that are born in our inner universe, then the creativity, to me, is the ground where I place those seeds. On their own, these seeds are wonderful, but they will not be able to blossom fully in this world if not placed in a fertile soil. It is very difficult to find the right place for the future garden without knowing what you actually want to plant there. But when you trust the moment and you have the seeds, you will always find a place for them—perhaps, the seeds themselves know. Nature itself will ensure that they grow strong and flourish.

By allowing myself these live, spontaneous reactions and trusting them, it was as if I discovered a portal into a limitless creative space, where there is a place for my entire creative energy. I felt that around my Inner Home there was enough space and fertile soil for any of my ideas, wishes, desires, and endeavors. Most importantly, there was no need to fight for these lands, no need to wait for the right moment, or accumulate anything to own them. The space is free and ready to accept these divine seeds to grow a wonderful blossoming garden. I know for sure that these seeds were born in my Inner Home, in my true, safe, and free place. They did not come to me from the outside, were not copied from others (however beautiful the others may have been) and were not a part of some greater industrial production of creative seeds.

I know that these expressions of spontaneity and creativity are natural and true. They occur not in the name of something, but rather they are Life itself, the Highest Creation, and that is where their value lies for me.

This message from my Inner Housekeeper helps keep me on my spontaneous path:

You started with a spontaneous, divine spark. It is the essence of your whole being. When you allow yourself to release this spark, it becomes a real and natural seed, a true part of your inner nature. By trusting your spontaneity, you can discover your true potential, your inner life, your Inner Home. It may take time to turn this seed into a flower— a full new creation. But if you visit your inner garden of spontaneity and creativity every day, it becomes your life practice, the way of life. Gradually, your Inner Home will begin to fill with the scents and colors emanating from this beautiful garden.

On the Way to My Roots and Being Grounded

No flower on Earth can completely flourish and open if it is plucked from the ground and its roots are torn away. Many know this truth. We know that Nature functions this way, and we accept its laws as a given, without arguing or doubting them. So why, when it comes to ourselves, the connection between the soil and our roots is so frequently disrupted or even denied? Why do we separate ourselves from Nature and its wise laws, thus denying an opportunity to bloom and open up fully?

I am used to feel unstable in this world! Sometimes I feel myself like a light feather that can be blown away with the slightest breeze. When swaying from side to side, it seems that no force exists that could pull me down to the ground and give me a chance to simply stand in place and rest. Sometimes, it is the opposite—I feel like a centuries-old mountain, impossible to move.

At some point in my life, I discovered that I frequently (and unconsciously) separated myself from the force of the earth, from nature, its wide and unconditional love and support. Here it is, under my feet, so strong and wise, but I turn away from it, not noticing, not feeling grounded.

My relationship with earth and my own roots did not develop easily. I do not think it was because when I was a child, no one around me was talking about the wise forces of Nature or taught me to treat it with attention and respect. The truth is, I never wanted to ground myself, never wished to stand firmly on the ground with my own two feet. In my internal reasoning, being grounded meant being typical, ordinary, drowning in everyday problems. Moreover, a person who stood firmly on the ground, in my understanding, was completely devoid of the feeling of flight, freedom, or creativity. That is, I sincerely believed that if I came closer to the ground and everything earthly, I would lose my ability to float in my imagination to the mysterious worlds and realities.

This feeling of flight was the little that I was able to retain in my complicated process of growing up; that is why I was holding onto it and was not ready to risk it. Having matured a little bit, I submerged myself in spiritual practices and those of developing spiritual abilities in me that greatly enriched and broadened my inner world. Yet, everything that related to the grounded, real, material processes caused an enormous anxiety and even fear in me. Essentially, I was floating farther and higher away, feeling myself as a highly-spiritual and free person, all the while suffering from a sensation of insecurity, instability, and detachment from the reality that surrounded me. I felt my infinite loneliness, like a lost comet in the space—it is very special but has no idea where and why it is flying. I did not know in what reality I would end up the next moment, where and when I would land. It seemed to me that in this way, I was relinquishing control and allowing life to lead me.

But today, I see that it was precisely then that I was trying so hard to control everything that happened to me, just because I was feeling deeply insecure and detached from life itself. In so many ways, I was missing out on my life, as if watching it from the sidelines. However, I was not neutrally observing myself from the inside, but rather from the outside; separately from my body, my reality, my inner ground—essentially, separate from my Inner Home. It helped me survive, but not live. Back then, I thought that most of what was happening to me was a spiritual, free, and creative flow. Now, looking back, I realize that very often it was a dissociation dictated by the fear of seeing the truth and really being present here and now, in my Inner Home.

My process of grounding began gradually when my children were born. They needed me here and now, with my full attention and concentration, and they needed a mother who was not free-floating. Precisely because of my children, I was able to finally understand what it meant to have my feet planted firmly on the ground and feel a connection with my roots. I was most amazed at the fact that while running all the daily home errands that any mother would, I felt an incredible spiritual boost, even in the most difficult times. It was exactly this first experience that united my feelings of flying and being grounded and turned me in the direction of connecting *inside me* the forces of heaven and earth. For me, it became a long return to the forces of Nature, earth, and all living things that exist on this planet. Most importantly, to my own grounding.

During those moments and subsequently, I realized that first and foremost I am a person who walks on this earth. I have a choice to use gravity either as a restriction that does not let me fly, or as the strength that gives my body support and stability. This allows my inner spiritual flight to take place, without losing the perception of time, space, and connection with reality and other people. It is this very connection with the earth and my roots that gives me a chance to open up and blossom. I became a part of greater Nature, allowing my inner nature to follow the wise laws of the greater one and fill me with strength and maternal care.

This connection with everything living allows me to feel myself a grounded spiritual person. I feel my connection with the previous generations that walked this path before me—it is as if they are standing behind me, sustaining my spine, helping me walk through life with my back straight and head up. I feel my connection with the forces of nature and the universe around me that are always ready to guide and support me on my journey. I feel a connection with the higher spiritual worlds, with my imagination and my soul. I can feel my own body and the processes that happen in it. This grounding connection is much more stable, strong, and safe for me and those around who depend on me.

The message from my Inner Heart Companion:

When I stand on the ground, on Mother Earth, I am connected to my roots. I feel my heart beating steadily and calmly. I hear my thoughts passing through. I feel my body, my presence and my center. I can feel myself. I can feel grounded, rooted, natural and free. I feel safe and connected to my Inner Home and the world around me, while enjoying the free, creative and enlightening flow.

On the Way to Spirituality

For me, spirituality is, first and foremost, the acceptance of self as a miracle of creation, an infinite unexplored planet that is not limited by the body, mind, and emotions. It is faith in one's own divinity, unity with one's soul, and trust in that force. Today, many call this kind of experience *a spiritual awakening,* an awakening of spirit or soul. Yet, I think that spirituality is more than a one-time awakening. As I see it, it is a practice of every day awakening. It is the recognition of one's self above all as a spiritual creature, and only then human. Coming to that realization, yields an acceptance of miracles, higher powers, blessings, signs, knowledge, depth, and creation inside one's self.

I have come to see that my own spirituality does not lie in different spiritual practices that I might do by rote. Nor does it mean that I speak or act in a virtuous manner, or pray and meditate in a specific way. My spirituality is alive for me when I hear my inner God, trust it, and follow my own higher purpose, that I have long searched for and found.

As I become more of a spiritual person (a person of spirit), it is important for me to accept all of my inner universe and explore and inhabit it over the course of my life. I do not need to understand all of who I am or everything that is going on within my inner universe—that is impossible. Just so, it is

239

impossible to know and understand all the laws and mysteries of the universe that surround us. So rather than wrestling with questions I can never have answers for, I simply accept as given an immense colorful and diverse world that lives inside me. The same way, I truly believe that each person is not a half or a quarter, but a whole, complete, autonomous universe. Just this thought brings great joy into my life.

Looking over the path toward my inner spirituality, I see that, luckily or unluckily, I did not grow up in a religious or spiritually-focused environment. Currently, Russia has in many ways returned to its religious roots. But in the time of my childhood, especially in Siberia, there was no talking about spirituality at all. There was science, culture, intellectual development. But no one around me would even mention spiritual growth, religion, or soul connection, except from the Russian literature, which was very fulfilling but hard to understand at a young age. At some point, I learned that I was Jewish, and I became very interested in learning about the Jewish traditions. Later I realized that what had interested me was not the actual traditions, but the opportunity to find a path to my soul. So, it was in this way that my soul began to speak to me, appear for me.

At the age of 16 I moved to Israel, a country that, contrary to Russia, was completely immersed in religious beliefs and traditions. I quickly felt that religion in its traditional expression was not my path, and continued my search for spirituality. After a few years, I became fascinated by the books concerning metaphysics, energy, spiritual awakening. I read them voraciously and felt that I was getting closer to something important. I was sure that soon I would discover a very weighty and essential secret or piece of knowledge in one of those books or at a spiritual workshop. Maybe, I would meet a teacher who would finally open to me the mystery of the universe.

Such a magical meeting did indeed occur, but not at all as I had imagined. I gave birth to my son. After spending a year with him, watching him, and uniting with his pure and true soul, I, for the first time, felt my own soul, my higher purpose, and the forces of my soul. For me, that year was the best spiritual university from which I could ever graduate. At that time, we did not have a TV (we were not purchasing one purposely), and I spent almost all the time alone with my son, listening only to music, going for walks with him, feeding him, and enjoying our little, but so full world.

I am not trying to paint some perfect picture. Of course, I would get tired, frustrated, and sleep-deprived like any young mother. But despite all the physical discomfort, my soul was singing. I literally heard that singing from within. I remember clearly this feeling of happiness and freedom that was not coming from the heart, but from my very center, wrapping me from head to toe. I remember how I looked at my son and felt that the most important event in my life had already occurred, and because of that my soul felt very calm. It seemed that everything else would now definitely fall into place because I had fulfilled my higher purpose—to be a mother to my son. And therefore, the beginning of the journey had been marked and this path surely would bring me Home to myself.

And, it was really so, it was the truth of my soul, of my inner universe. I think that every woman, with the birth of her child, goes through some kind of a spiritual awakening, simply because inside her a new soul is born that necessarily influences the mother's soul toward awakening or even rebirth. But, I am not sure that every woman feels a safe awakening of her own soul. This would be so, especially if she did not have any opportunity to connect to it before and now is also responsible for someone else's.

Another element emerges with motherhood, that is not necessarily blissful, yet still awakening. Working on an emotional level with many mothers and having my own motherhood experience, I found that very often, upon taking on the role of a mother, we consciously and unconsciously arouse our childhood traumas. When this happens, we come to be overwhelmed with heavy feelings that we did not deal with before. Sometimes these unfinished or unprocessed matters simply cover our soul with their own weight, and it falls asleep more deeply. And a mother, who feels this repression, may tell herself not to worry, "I will raise the children, and then think about my own soul."

In my case, the role of mother gave me faith—faith in my soul, in myself, in my truth—to look for answers not in the books on maternity and child rearing, but inside me. I learned to feel my child and respect his inner, separate-from-me universe; to rely on my intuition and inner wisdom and on the wisdom of his inner universe. I think that precisely because I saw in him such a strong, free, and wise soul I was able to believe in the existence of my own.

So, as I noted above, this is precisely there where my conscious spiritual living began. When I recognized this, I started to listen deeply to my personal inner divine source, to my higher powers, and to my soul. It does not mean at all that I separated from the outside world with its laws and traditions. On the contrary, I no longer needed to climb a mountain alone, go to a monastery, or meditate for hours. I learned that I could be among people, living and enjoying all the earthly happiness, and yet feel myself spiritually filled and fulfilled.

My journey to such spirituality continues even today because the closer I am to my soul, the more I learn about its true meaning and higher purpose. It opens itself to me, sharing its secrets, powers, and knowledge. Like any soul, it is filled with unconditional love, and hence it does not pressure me, does not rush me; rather, it gives me a chance to hear my own truth only when all the human in me (my mind, my nervous system, my body) is ready for it. And I have long since learned to trust its pace and believe that today I know

243

exactly what I need to know today. No more, no less. I trust The Way to my own true spirituality.

Message from my Inner Housekeeper:

Today, your inner spiritual fire flares up from the natural trees and woods that you found in your inner nature. It takes time to find the right, authentic wood for the inner fire, it takes time to discover the right way to kindle the fire and to keep the flame. It takes a lot of patience, trust and faith in your own divine spark that will eventually burst into a warm, strong and true spiritual fire.

Becoming an Owner of My Inner Home

No matter what your destination is right now,
you are always on The Way Home.

On the Way to Co-authorship

Somehow, I have always felt the power of holding the Author's pen to record a true inner story, without trying to control or change it. But until recently, I have not seen this role as my conscious choice. I did not realize that I am not only the author but also the owner of my inner truth. And this is the only thing that I truly own. I had tried to own the life around me instead of the life within, in my Inner Home. Very often, I experienced myself in two opposite and extreme states: I should be in full charge and control of life, or I am powerless and cannot lead myself anywhere. With time, I realized that no matter how much I wish to possess irrefutable rights to create my own life, I cannot ignore the Highest Author and Creator, who can end my life story at any moment and turn the plot into a direction completely unexpected to me. No matter how much I wish sometimes to insist that everything in my life is a result of my own work and creation, I cannot overlook the fact that certain chapters of my life extend well beyond my imagination and were imagined and narrated by an Author of a much grander scale. Yet, the story is ingeniously simple.

I am in awe of the talent of this Higher Author and the ease with which He creates worlds and realities. I think it is this admiration and, at times worship, that drove me sometimes to kneel and say

246

humbly, "No matter what, I will never reach Your level. I am learning and working hard; I am trying. And yet, I remain only a copy, a careless student, a mediocre talent who wastes her potential. I am tired of being useless. This is why I am giving the authorship to You. I ask You, please write what you want, and I will follow your plot, without arguing." In moments like this, I would finally feel relief and able to breathe and relax. But then, my inner truthful author starts imagining what this Higher Author might be feeling. I project that, just like many humans, He may be perturbed when someone takes advantage of Him or that, perhaps, even He is not ready to complete this work by Himself, alone. I further think He may also need support and the joy of co-creation. He, too, needs a full-time partner, and not a slave or admiring fanatic. And I realize that this genius Author had a reason to bring me into this world; I was not to become a puppet in His Theater of Life. This genius Author, as I have come to know Him, has no desire to dominate, rule, and decide. He is looking for a co-author—one who is thoughtful, searching and unique in his own way. One who can own his inner authorship and be ready for true co-creation. And, only when I realized and accepted myself as a true owner of my Inner Home and the author of my inner life story, was I able to accept the reality that I am also a co-author of the story of my life. I recognized that I am not the main author, as I wanted to believe, and not the passive spectator, who does not have any effect on the story.

Co-authorship like any co-creation is very challenging and complicated. It requires much patience, respect, openness, confidence, trust, and persistence; acceptance of one´s uniqueness and that of the others; acceptance of a Unity; and, of course, acceptance of boundaries and limits. This does not come right away, it is not a talent. It is a skill. It is an ability. It is a journey and a process. My journey to co-authorship only became possible when I assumed full responsibility for my part of the work. But in order to feel responsible, without feeling like it is an imposed chore, I needed to understand and recognize it, to tell myself the untold parts of my inner story. Only then, did this responsibility become a conscious choice. That is why I had to clarify my inner story, my inner life experience, describe the characters I met throughout my journey, fill in the blanks and say the unsaid, feel the unfelt, experience what I had not lived to the fullest. Most importantly, I had to separate all the intertwined stories and plots of others from my own, the one I lived through. I had to tell it my way, in my unique style, with my co-author hand.

Now, looking back to this journey of releasing my true inner story, I can tell that this is a totally different experience than to hear my story as told by someone else. The turning point on this journey was when I let myself believe that I was given that Creator's pen from the very beginning and not just by anybody, but by the Highest Author Himself! He put in an effort, dedicated entire pages to me, freed up the space for creating. In the end, He offered me His services, "I give you life, so please try to add something of your own so that it is unlike anyone else's, so that it is in your own handwriting. Maybe we will create something new, add a new color into the grand picture of the world."

No matter how hard I tried to refuse it or to simply ignore it, passing it in my thoughts to someone else or taking it away from someone who I thought had stolen it from me, this Author's Pen was and is always with me. It is inside me, and therefore cannot disappear, get stolen or lost. It is in my Inner Home, in the very place where I keep all the truest and most precious parts of myself. It is always safe, because no external force can break through my inner codes, passwords, and locks; no external force knows my hideaways. Only I know them. And this is why only I can choose and decide that the time has finally come to fully own this Author's tool and take on the role of a co-creator. I will not say that this is an easy task. It is sometimes exhausting; sometimes selfless, and sometimes requiring courage, strength, and will. This work is also filled with the excitement of creation, inspiration, magical and vital energy.

Recognizing and owning my inner life experiences, sharing them and acknowledging my responsibility for continuing my own story, makes me the author in the highest sense of this word. Accepting my role as a co-creator gives me a chance to express my inner voice and stand out among the chorus of millions of others. I get an opportunity to influence, create, fulfill, to give and receive. I get a chance to share all of who I am, to share my story, my experience, my understanding of the plot, and my author's talent. Each day I hone my authorship skills and learn the wisdom of co-creation. I am learning to keep balance, without taking on too much or negating my authorship. I am learning to be a partner to the Highest Author and Creator. Today I can be a true owner of my consciousness, my feelings, my imagination and creativity, my truth, my Inner Home.

My Inner Housekeeper tells me:

One of my main jobs on this journey was to wipe out all the shame and blame talk that was accumulated within, helping you to clear the vision. Then you were able to see your truth clearly and record it as it is, without judging, scoring or distorting it. You did not have to analyze yourself or recollect all the events that happened to you. You just needed to recognize your true feelings, to find your true ideas and dreams, to connect to the parts of your natural self and to own them as a part of your Inner Home.

Because when, and only when, you become an owner of your inner truth, you can then co-create your true and unique life story.

On the Way to Being in Service

Everything within a human being is built on mutual aid and cooperation—be it physiological, spiritual, emotional, or intellectual. None of these processes or elements can exist autonomously. The meaning and value of our inner nature depends on how aligned and synchronized the processes are among themselves. If the organs of our body had minds that could think, I believe that no organ would consider itself to be more important, valuable, or deserving than the others. None would have doubts about serving one another in the name of a common good. Each would know for certain what it is responsible for and would fulfill its duty without having doubts, feeling shy, or being proud of what it does. When I ponder this interdependency within the context of our body, it seems natural and obvious. It seems that this natural balance is programmed in us by Nature itself, without any need to create it artificially and expend a large effort to preserve it.

Yet, I know many persons who are confused about mutual aid and serving for each other's good, understanding the overall balance of the universe. I know that my own confusion affected my inner nature and there were times when it did not react naturally and did not take care of this balance. It was at those moments that many parts of my inner world suddenly stopped fulfilling their functions and started to get

251

preoccupied with other matters completely out of their domain. Therefore, I started to ask myself honest questions, knowing that answering them would bring back the ability to be natural in my service and clear in my respective roles for each other's good and overall balance. Some of those questions were: What does it truly mean to serve another's good? How do I get a clear, deep, and natural answer to this question? And how do I join with the common flow of universal balance, precisely, freely, and naturally?

My attitude toward mutual aid and overall serving of whatever principles and whomever I meet has changed much throughout my life. When I was little, I heard many moral rules about helping the weak, serving the country or the common good, about being helpful. I heard it from the adults around me, from books and movies. I remember that I really liked all those ideas, and they would make me feel a certain awe and respect. Yet, as I got older, I found fewer and fewer life examples of such true and heartfelt serving. I am not saying that there were no such people. But for some reason, during my teen years, I did not meet many who would do it sincerely and naturally. Some people talked about the importance of helping each other, yet, it seemed that they chose, as the subject of their help, someone who did not ask for it, while not helping their own children, who needed them, as if on purpose. Or those people, who were barely staying afloat, would drop everything and run to the rescue of someone just like them, lost and deprived, only to sink themselves and the object of their help. Of course, there were cases in which they would happily make it all together, but much of the time it would only worsen their own condition and convince them of life's injustice. There were also people who, on the contrary, wanted to serve only the successful and healthy, turning away from misfortune, anxiety, and unpredictability. There were even those who served their cause truly and faithfully but considered serving their own families to be a humiliation and a waste of time. Overall, this entire process seemed to me completely unbalanced, unnatural, and often even hypocritical. Every time I helped someone not because I felt that I truly wanted to give and share, but because it was "the right thing to do", it was as if I became diminished in my own eyes. Yet, when I decided to be honest with myself and not offer help when it did not feel true, I felt as a selfish egoist and was tormented by the feeling of guilt. Overall, everything was complicated and seemed twisted and upside down. Meanwhile, all I wanted was simplicity, just as when I was a child.

I remember that in high school I got so tied up in this question that I started to feel completely useless. I wanted to help and serve, but felt that I did not know whom and how I could help. That is, I had no desire to lie and be a hypocrite; but to be truly of service I needed to know myself and my strengths— and I did not. So, I was hiding my head in the sand and acted as if all those ideals had nothing to do with me.

253

Later, my children came to my rescue in this question. As soon as my first son was born, and then my daughter, I suddenly realized that in my life there was and would not be anything more important. At that time, I felt with all my heart that the main purpose of my service to this world was being a mom, whom each of her children needed. Having found this ultimate role that would give me worth, I had no idea that such honest and sincere serving would eventually lead me to becoming a therapist, that I can be really helpful in what is completely natural to me—that is, psychotherapy. This realization came to me not because of a feeling of my own greatness or even talent, but because I was able to help myself, my family, and those around me, in various psychological aspects. This was exactly what gave me the confidence in my own strength and a sincere desire to share it. It was born very naturally and freely, precisely when I was ready to start serving outside of my own family—I was lucky.

But even upon entering the realm of therapy, which seemed to be built upon serving and helping people, I still had my doubts. First, all my inner theory was based on the premise that everyone should be responsible for helping himself. Being in the role of a therapist, I felt pressure from myself. On the one hand, I wanted to help and sometimes even rescue; but on the other, I believed that no one but that person himself is his best healing agent. At the same time, I already felt the strength and desire to be with my

254

patient naturally and freely, uncovering my abilities and true potential, thus helping my client open up to himself and recover his essence and strength. Yet, when I allowed myself just to be present and true, without having an agenda at all, everything would start to work by itself. I felt myself in the right place. And at the same time, on some deep level, I felt as if the truth of my serving was still not completely uncovered for me.

Already living in America, I remember when one wonderful therapist and psychodramatist, John Olesen, said at one of his training sessions on psychodrama, "Do not try to be better. Simply remember that when we are natural and present, we are already in service of each other." That was when something inside me clicked, and the whole picture came together at once. I felt, with every cell of my body that when I am true and natural, just the way I am in this moment, I am in the best service that I can be. That is, when I try being useful, try to help and serve, I take away my own opportunity to be my true self and, therefore, am not serving the common balance. At the same time, when I rely on the idea that everything inside me is already in tune with this balance and mutual aid, everything starts to work on its own, clearly and naturally.

I know that I would not be able to believe again in this simple truth if I had not gone through this journey of doubt, denial, questions, answers, and much learning and practice. Only after I had tried an array of options, was I able to appreciate the simplest one: When I am natural and true in all my expressions and processes, I serve myself and those around me.

Now I can see that this realization most likely brought me to this time, in which I feel that I have found my true service to this world—sharing the idea of the Inner Home and everything that comes with this vision. I feel confident about this particular serving because it came to me naturally, as if it were always there. Each time I talk, write or share this vision in any way, I feel true, balanced and fulfilled. I feel that I am doing the right thing, that I am in a right place, that I am truly in service for others and give my piece to the common universal balance of mutual aid. I feel at Home!

Message from my Inner Heart Companion:

I do not need to understand how exactly all this works and what exactly my role is in preserving the overall balance. Just as I will probably never fully understand why at this moment my heart is beating faster, my mind is drawing a specific picture, my soul is quiet, and my stomach is rumbling. But I know that there is meaning and wisdom in all of this, whether I understand it or not. I believe that my inner Nature, just like the one around me, knows what it is doing—and I trust it. When I allow myself to trust and give freedom of service to my inner Nature, everything becomes easy, true and natural, just as when I was a child.

This is how it should be in a home, where everything is based on mutual aid and a common balance—in a true Inner Home.

On the Way to Sharing My Gifts

Let us imagine this hypothetical situation: Before it is born, your soul stands before God who blesses it prior to its long journey. The Creator tells your soul, "I wish to bestow upon you a precious and important gift. With it, you will always remember me, you will always be sure of your path on Earth, you will feel joy and get strength from this gift. The Person in whom you will live will develop this gift however he or she wants and through it discover within so many other hidden treasures! And then you, Soul, will able to be truly happy and free!

"But I have a request for you, also. This gift is too vast for any one person and any one soul. Therefore, I am asking you to share it generously with all the people around. Do not worry, your Person will always have plenty. The more you will share this gift, the more it will grow inside and make you even richer. The difficult part is that when you are born, the Person will not know about this gift or about this request of mine. Most likely, the Person will be afraid, will hesitate and hide away from this gift. He or she can surround him or herself with circumstances and people who will put obstacles on his or her journey to discovering this gift. Yet, with every day, it will be more and more difficult to keep inside. The Person may become irascible, mean, and even dangerous to himself or herself and those around. There is,

258

unfortunately, nothing I can do to help you. Only when the Person in whom you live will have the courage to share this gift with at least one living being, his or her life will be filled with wonders that will help you to uncover my gift and truly bask in its glory.

"I know that you, Soul, will not forget about this gift. You will remember it and try with all your power to remind the Person, inside which you will live, about it. But only he or she can take this step forward and share the gift. This Person must overcome everything human that is in him or her and give you a chance to show your treasure. The moment he or she does that, we all will sing our song of blessings, and you will be able to sing with us, too. The Person will surely hear our song, and will feel truly blessed and gifted!"

Since I was a little girl, I have always felt the presence of this gift, its inner weight and some sort of inner responsibility. I did not know what it was, but I felt that there was a special meaning inside of me, a riddle that was hidden deep inside, for which I needed to find an answer. I felt that without discovering and opening up to this gift I would never be truly at Home with myself. Inside me there was always some sort of incompleteness that left me with an innuendo or feeling of dissatisfaction, disappointment, and resentment toward myself. I often hurried and forced myself to figure out who I was and what I could share with this world. But the pressure never helped—on the contrary, it only hindered my process of opening up. By rushing and squeezing some kind of result out of myself, I only clamped up more inside and got farther from my inner gift, only letting out the mechanical, soulless results. Most importantly, the opportunity to share my true treasure with someone was fading away.

Finally, at one point, it seemed to me completely impossible to dig out my true self, much less share it with the world around me. Luckily for me, my soul kept calling and showing me the ways in which I could—albeit slowly, one little bit at a time—open up my inner gift and feel at least a temporary relief. I remember how I spent hours just sitting and watching my little son dance. To him, it was important that I witnessed his artistic search, and with each performance I saw how his inner gift was becoming more open and obvious to him and the people around. I was so happy to be that person for him, with whom he could openly share this gift. But I was even happier when I realized that, by looking at him, inside me something was awakening, opening, and singing. Even though it was still my son's song, and not my own, when I heard it, my faith was growing stronger that something like that could one day happen to me.

One day I caught myself thinking that, sadly, in my childhood, there was no one with whom I could share my gift. This is not about who is to blame; rather, what to do about it. I realized that the main person receiving this gift from my soul today should be me. I myself can not only listen to these hints that my soul is giving me, but I can also believe in them. I can begin to share my feelings, dreams, ideas, and aspirations because only I can give my soul a chance to express this gift. I can be the first to witness the revelation of my gift in my Inner Home—just as treasure hunters follow the lead, without losing faith and hope to find the hidden treasure, even though no one else believes that it is possible. So, when I myself started to believe in this gift bestowed upon my soul and set out to search for it inside me, almost miraculously a person appeared in my life with whom I could share the most intimate parts of my inner life. This person became my best friend and, as of this writing, we have been friends for over seventeen years. By sharing my most secret dreams, desires, and spiritual impulses with her and feeling her support, I was opening more to my soul. In my life, truly wonderful 'accidents' were occurring that helped my gift reveal itself to me and to those around.

The miracle of this gift is that it fills my life with purpose and allows me to share it with others, without emptying myself, on the contrary, I gain and grow so much. I more often can hear the song of blessings that my soul, together with the Higher Power, is singing to me. And I truly hope that increasingly more souls will join this song, that many more human beings will share their gifts one with another and will feel truly blessed and gifted.

This message comes from my Inner Heart Companion:

When I generously share my gifts, I feel that my Inner Home is lit and plentiful. When I reveal my gifts, I can overcome the human complexes, fears and limitations because my soul is leading me, and I trust its journey. I accept, with respect and awe, the role of a person who can witness the revelation of such gifts in the people close to me. By sharing my inner gifts, I feel a connection with all the divine that is inside and around me. I consequently, feel true about my journey on this Earth. I feel Home with who I am.

Author's Biography

Vlada Zapesotsky was born in Siberia, Russia into a highly creative family. Her mother, Irena Deitch, is a TV director and her father, Genady Deitch, a journalist and newspaper editor. When she was just sixteen years-old, she decided to leave Russia, by herself, for Israel. Being a Russian Jew, she believed Israel to be her true home. While there, Vlada studied journalism and at the age of nineteen she became an Israeli cultural commentator for one of the largest International Russian Channels. After a few years, she worked in the field of movie production, taking different roles of scenarist, director's assistant, and producer. Concurrently, she was studying Educational Psychology, a field she found highly interesting, and soon discovered Psychodrama. Becoming impressed with its depth and efficacy in helping people deal with problems, Vlada continued studying this method. After graduation, Vlada worked in Barzilai University Medical Center, as a Psychodrama Creative Art Therapist.

In 2014, Vlada moved to the Bay Area in California with her husband and two children. After receiving American credentials as a practitioner in Psychodrama, Sociometry and Group psychotherapy, she founded a center of healing and creativity, *The Way Home*, where she leads workshops, trainings, and experiential and educational sessions and courses in English, Hebrew and Russian. At this center, Vlada has developed her own healing vision and creative action model, *The Way Home-to Your True Self*, serving people on a personal and professional level, with a focus on trauma issues.

Vlada can be reached by email: <u>vladlenad@gmail.com</u>.

76493654R00155

Made in the USA
San Bernardino, CA
12 May 2018